SBJC

AUG 2023

 **W9-COO-491**

INDIAN RHINOCEROS CALF

SABLE KIT

NATIONAL GEOGRAPHIC
KiDS

ULTIMATE MAMMAL-PEDIA

THE MOST COMPLETE MAMMAL REFERENCE EVER

STEPHANIE WARREN DRIMMER

NATIONAL GEOGRAPHIC

WASHINGTON, D.C.

CONTENTS

LONG-HAIRED SPIDER MONKEY

VIRGINIA OPOSSUM

SUMATRAN TIGER

GIRAFFE

ZEBRAS

WALRUS

RED PANDA

MEERKAT

FOREWORD

Mammals are some of the most fascinating, strong, and complex animals on our planet. They originated on Earth more than 150 million years ago and even lived during the age of dinosaurs. We humans are lucky to be mammals—and we're in really good company.

Humans love their fellow mammals. We learn about them in zoos, plan family trips to see them in the wild, cuddle with toy versions of them, tell stories about them, and even share our homes with some of them. From the moment that I, as a young girl, saw my first nature show on television, I knew that studying the biggest, strongest, most ferocious mammals in the world was the job that I wanted to have. I'll never forget watching tigers in the jungles of South Asia slink across my television screen and knowing that I would do whatever it took to one day be able to work with these amazing creatures.

I'm not a tiger expert today, but I have dedicated my career as a wildlife ecologist to studying and protecting bears, lions, primates, and other amazing mammals all over the world. And I can't imagine having any other job! I'm best known for my work with large carnivorous mammals, but I've also developed a pretty good affinity for some of the smaller critters—the ones that are so obscure, and sometimes completely hidden, that it can be hard to know a lot about them or to even find them in the wild.

LIONS

A tremendous amount of diversity exists within the taxonomic class Mammalia. In *Ultimate Mammalpedia,* you'll learn creepy-crawly, nitty-gritty, weird, fascinating, sweet, mind-blowing facts about this planet's amazing diversity of mammals. **This book will take you from the familiar to the exotic and everywhere in between while you meet some of the most amazing animals on this planet!**

BROWN BEARS

Dr. Rae Wynn-Grant
large carnivore ecologist and expert consultant for *Ultimate Mammalpedia*

INTRODUCTION

They live all around you. Some scamper and scurry across the ground. Others dig beneath your feet. Still others leap from tree to tree, swim in lakes and seas, or even fly through the air. They are the mammals, and they are perhaps the most diverse group of animals on Earth.

You'd have to enter the oceans to enter the realm of fish, or shrink to a tiny size to grasp the world of insects. But mammals are more familiar to us. Many, such as squirrels, rats, and coyotes, might share your backyard. You may have seen some that normally live far away, such as tigers and elephants, in zoos. Others, like cats and dogs, might even live with you in your home! And of course, you are a mammal, too.

But the world of mammals holds many secrets. How did they come to rule a planet once dominated by dinosaurs? How did they take on such different forms as an elk, a porcupine, and a dolphin? How do they find food, take shelter, and raise their young?

This book will answer all these questions about mammals, and many more. **Get ready to become an expert on all things furry!**

Stephanie Warren Drimmer
science writer and author of
Ultimate Mammalpedia

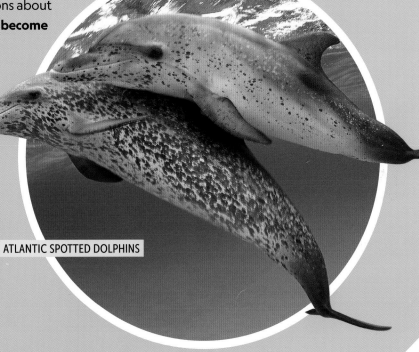

ATLANTIC SPOTTED DOLPHINS

CHAPTER **ONE**

THE WORLD OF
MAMMALS

WHAT IS A MAMMAL?

FLYING FOX

They wiggle their whiskers and stomp their hooves. They groom their companions and bare their razor-sharp teeth. They move in all sorts of ways: by running, climbing, scurrying, swinging, digging, swimming, hopping—and even flying! Some munch on plants, others chase down prey. They can be as tiny as a shrew or as big as a blue whale. They are the mammals.

There are more than 6,000 species of mammals on Earth. Lions, kangaroos, monkeys, and dolphins may look totally different from one another, but they all belong to this animal group. What is it that makes a mammal a mammal and not a bird, a fish, or another type of creature?

There are four qualities that all mammals share: All have hair or fur. In an animal such as the sea otter, this can take the form of a thick, luxurious coat. But even slick-skinned dolphins have hair: It's present only when they are first born and falls out soon after. Mammals also have mammary glands, which produce milk that females use to feed their young. They have a hinged jaw that attaches directly to their skull. (Animals such as birds and reptiles have jaws that attach to another bone.) And mammals have three tiny bones in their ears that help transmit sound.

These qualities might sound familiar: Humans also have hair, are nursed with milk, and have a hinged jaw and ear bones. That's because humans are a type of mammal, too! From whales to warthogs to wombats—and to you—mammals are some of the most adaptable, widespread, and fascinating animals on Earth.

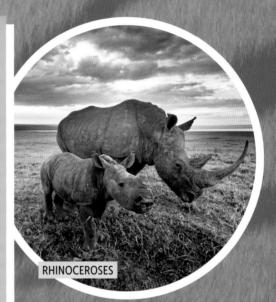

RHINOCEROSES

PRAIRIE DOGS

AFRICAN LION

That's Fact-tastic!

The **LARGEST MAMMAL,** the **BLUE WHALE,** is **80 MILLION TIMES HEAVIER** than the **SMALLEST MAMMAL,** the **KITTI'S HOG-NOSED BAT.** This tiny flier is also known as the bumblebee bat because it's about the same size as the buzzing insect.

CHIMPANZEES

BLUE WHALE

Most mammals care for their young after they are born. Some, such as **CHIMPANZEES, LIVE** with their **MOTHER** for about **SIX YEARS.**

AFRICAN ELEPHANT CALF

MAKING A
HOME

Mammals have evolved, or changed very slowly over time, to live in nearly every habitat on Earth, and they can be found on every one of Earth's continents and in every ocean. Many have adaptations that help them live in places where other animals might not be able to survive. A fennec fox's (p. 56) oversize ears, for example, help release extra heat from the fox's body, keeping it cool in its Sahara home. The layer of blubber under a polar bear's (p. 194) skin acts like a blanket, keeping the bear warm even when it takes a dip in frigid Arctic waters.

One reason mammals can live in so many different environments is that nearly all of them are endothermic, or "warm-blooded." While exothermic, or "cold-blooded," animals like snakes and lizards must warm their bodies by basking in the sun, endothermic animals have bodies that can create their own heat. They have an ability to keep their body temperature at a constant level, no matter the temperature of their environment. This helps mammals survive in both hot and cold places.

Many people think *all* mammals are endothermic, but this isn't true. Though there are no exothermic mammals in the same way as snakes or

FENNEC FOX

That's **Fact-tastic!**

Most mammals live on land. But **SOME LAND DWELLERS ALMOST NEVER TOUCH** the **GROUND.** Many mammals, including **SUGAR GLIDERS** and monkeys, are **ARBOREAL,** meaning that they spend nearly all their lives in the **TREETOPS.**

SUGAR GLIDER

WHALES LIVE in EVERY OCEAN on EARTH.

HUMPBACK WHALE

BROWN BEAR

lizards, some mammals are what experts call heterothermic: Sometimes they control their own body temperature, and other times their temperature varies with the environment. Some mouse lemurs (p. 223), for example, spend more than nine hours a day in a state called torpor: Their heart rates and metabolisms slow down, and their body temperature drops to less than 45°F (7°C). Some mammals, such as brown bears, spend the whole winter in torpor. This adaptation allows mammals to conserve energy, helping them survive in places where there otherwise wouldn't be enough food to fuel them.

Because mammals inhabit so much of the planet, many face tough competition for food. To survive, they have incredible adaptations that help them get enough resources: Giraffes (p. 74), for example, use their long necks to reach leaves that the shorter zebras and antelope that share their African savanna home can't get. Living in these wide-open grasslands forced these zebras and antelope to evolve tough hooves and long legs to outrun predators such as cheetahs—which in turn evolved great speed and slashing teeth and claws to help them capture their prey. Mammals' environments have shaped their bodies and behaviors—but mammals shape their environments, too! Elephants, for example, are known for uprooting trees to create open areas and for digging to make watering holes.

ROTHSCHILD'S GIRAFFES

13

FINDING FOOD

RACCOON

A **mammal's body works hard.** Keeping an animal's body at a constant temperature takes a lot of energy—never mind all the energy it takes to swing through the rainforest searching for fruit or chasing down insects to eat. All animals get the energy they need to fuel their bodies from their diet. And mammals' diets are as different from one another as their bodies and behaviors are.

Many mammals are carnivores, or meat-eaters. Carnivores can't digest plants well, and they must eat meat to survive. Carnivores include animals such as lions, tigers, and wolves. Animals such as hedgehogs, which hunt and eat insects, are also carnivores. Baleen whales—which filter tiny creatures called zooplankton out of the water—are carnivores, too! Many carnivores have large skulls with strong jaws adapted for snapping, holding tight to prey, and ripping and tearing meat. Some even have special upper and lower teeth that close together like scissors to slice through flesh. Generally, carnivores eat plant-eaters, but some also eat other carnivores.

Some mammals are omnivores. They are the most flexible eaters on the planet, able to digest both meat and plants. That makes them adaptable: When there isn't meat to be found, they can survive on foods such as fruit and fungi. Brown bears are omnivores that eat a diet of plants, berries, fish, and small mammals. Their long, strong claws can dig for grubs, pick bird eggs out of a nest, or snag a leaping salmon right out of the water. Other omnivorous mammals are raccoons, squirrels, and coyotes. Omnivores belong to different mammal orders, or groups.

Then there are the herbivores, or plant-eaters. These animals, which include flying foxes, horses, and kangaroos, eat only vegetation, such as fruits, leaves, grasses, and roots. Eating plants might not sound impressive, but much vegetation is very difficult to digest, and animals that can fuel their bodies with plants alone have large, flat teeth adapted for grinding up tough plant material. They also often have stomachs with multiple chambers that extract every bit of energy out of their food. Some herbivores, such as cows, even bring up their meals to chew and digest multiple times. This chewed material is called cud. Herbivores are an essential part of their ecosystems, because they take plant material and convert it into energy. When an herbivore is eaten by a carnivore, that energy travels up the food chain, fueling the entire ecosystem.

> Animals aren't the only carnivores: There are more than **600 SPECIES** of **CARNIVOROUS PLANTS!**

LION CUBS

COYOTE

That's Fact-tastic!

The **MAMMALIAN ORDER,** or group of mammals, known as **CARNIVORA** means **"FLESH DEVOURER"** in Latin, but not all members of Carnivora are carnivores. Some, such as **BEARS** and **COYOTES,** are actually **OMNIVORES** that **EAT BOTH PLANTS AND MEAT.**

BROWN BEAR

HUNTER OR HUNTED?

WHITE-TAILED DEER FAWN

The jaguar moves through the jungle on silent paws, its muscles rippling underneath its spotted coat. This sleek cat is a powerful predator that uses stealth to stalk its prey through the rainforest. A quick leap, a *SNAP* of the jaws, and the jaguar has its dinner. It will survive to hunt another day.

When you think of a predator, you might think of a large creature with tearing claws and snapping teeth. Some predators, such as jaguars, lions, and wolves, fit this description. But not all predators do: A predator is an animal that hunts other animals. Pygmy shrews (p. 64) weigh just a bit more than a penny, but they are ferocious predators that hunt down and gobble up insects. And not all predators are mammals: Many birds and even insects such as ladybugs are predators, too.

Predators are an important part of their ecosystems because they keep the populations of other animals in check. If lions disappeared, for example, the numbers of zebras and antelope might grow out of control, until there would be so many that there wouldn't be enough grass to feed them all. Some predators, such as foxes, eat plant-eaters such as rodents. Other predators, such as wolves, eat foxes. Wolves are apex predators, or the animals at the very top of their food chain.

PYGMY SHREW

RED FOX

JAGUAR

That's Fact-tastic!

PREDATORS OFTEN TARGET THE WEAKEST or **SLOWEST PREY** animals they can find. This behavior pushes prey animals to **EVOLVE** over time to become **STRONGER** and **FASTER.** In turn, predators must evolve to become stronger and faster themselves to survive.

GIANT ANTEATER

Prey animals are hunted and eaten by predators. Many have adaptations that help keep them from being eaten. Some, like meerkats, live in groups so that one member can be watching out for danger while the rest search for food. Other prey animals use camouflage: A baby deer's spots, for example, help conceal it in the dappled light of the forest floor. Some predators use camouflage, too. A tiger's stripes help it hide in the jungle so it can sneak up on its prey.

There are some mammals that can be predators one day and prey the next: Today, a chimpanzee might catch and eat a monkey; tomorrow, a leopard might eat the chimpanzee.

ANTEATERS are **PREDATORS.** Some have **TONGUES** as **LONG** as a human arm, which they use to **SLURP UP ANTS.**

FAMILY LIFE

ROTHSCHILD'S GIRAFFES

Baby giraffes experience one of the most dramatic births in the animal kingdom: Giraffe mothers give birth while standing, and their babies begin life by falling all the way to the ground! This may sound like a rude awakening, but the shock of the fall actually helps the little giraffe begin breathing and moving on its own. Within hours after they are born, baby giraffes can stand, eat, and walk.

Most mammal mothers are like giraffes: They carry their young inside their bodies. These unborn baby mammals get their food and oxygen through the placenta, a special organ that grows during each pregnancy. It is the only known organ that works this way. Animals that nourish their unborn young with a placenta are called placental mammals. Some placental mammals, like elephants and humans, usually have only one baby at a time—though sometimes they can have multiples. Other animals, like mice and dogs, have a whole litter of babies at once.

POLAR BEARS

POLAR BEARS ALMOST ALWAYS give birth to **TWINS.**

AFRICAN ELEPHANT CALF

That's Fact-tastic!

When a **BABY ELEPHANT** is born, other **FEMALES** in the **HERD HELP** it **STAND UP** and show it how to **NURSE**. When a new baby joins the herd, the adult elephants also **SLOW THEIR PACE** so that the little one doesn't get too **TIRED.**

EASTERN GRAY KANGAROOS

ECHIDNA

Not all mammal babies grow inside their mother's body. Marsupials—or mammals with pouches, such as kangaroos—don't have a placenta, and they carry their young in their bodies for only a short period of time. When marsupial babies are still very tiny and helpless, they crawl through their mother's fur to her pouch. There, they nurse, growing bigger and stronger on their mother's milk. When they've grown enough, they leave the pouch and explore the world.

Reptiles and birds lay eggs. Some mammals do, too! They are called monotremes. Monotremes live in New Guinea, mainland Australia, and Tasmania, and they include only two types of animals: the platypus and the echidna. Monotremes lay leathery eggs, similar to those of turtles. Once the eggs hatch, the babies nurse from their mothers. But monotreme mothers don't have nipples like other mammals do. Instead, they "sweat" milk from patches on their bellies!

RISE OF THE MAMMALS

From about 245 to 66 million years ago, dinosaurs ruled planet Earth. They and other remarkable reptiles occupied every bit of the globe. There were tiny dinosaurs, enormous dinosaurs, dinosaurs that hunted in herds, dinosaurs that swam in the seas—even dinosaur cousins called pterosaurs that flew through the air. But they weren't alone. Lurking in the shadows were the mammals.

The first mammals were small animals similar to modern shrews (p. 64). They were called the morganucodontids, and they appeared about 210 million years ago along with several other similar kinds of mammals.

Experts say these first mammals probably survived by eating insects as they slowly changed through evolution over the 145 million years that followed. But the ruling reptiles were bigger, faster, and stronger. Dinosaurs outcompeted the tiny mammals for food and shelter—and ate them, too. Because of this, early mammals never grew larger than about the size of a house cat.

But that all changed about 66 million years ago, when a rock the size of a city came shooting out of space and slammed into Earth. The impact created a 125-mile (200-km)-wide crater that can still be seen today under the ocean off the coast of Mexico. This set off

DUCK-BILLED DINOSAURS

HIPPOPOTAMUS

Some mammals that look **VASTLY DIFFERENT** from one another are **ACTUALLY RELATIVES**, such as **HIPPOS** and **WHALES.**

ZALAMBDALESTES

HUMPBACK WHALE

VIRGINIA OPOSSUM

MAMMAL ORIGINS

The shrewlike morganucodontids were among the earliest mammals to appear, about 210 million years ago. Their relatives split off to become the ancestors of the three groups of mammals alive today: monotremes, marsupials, and placental mammals.

a chain reaction that rocked the planet with earthquakes, fires, and mudslides, along with rising temperatures that roasted Earth for centuries. Nearly every living thing on the planet was killed—including nearly all the dinosaurs. (One dinosaur lineage survived and evolved to become today's birds.)

Among the animals that made it through were the mammals. With the dinosaurs gone, they could eat new kinds of foods and take over new areas without competition—and without getting eaten. Mammals quickly took over: Just 10 million years after the dinosaurs disappeared, mammals had already split into many lineages, including almost all 18 living groups, called orders. From tiny rodent-like animals, they grew, spread out, and changed into animals as varied as blue whales, brown bears, and bandicoots.

SAVED FROM EXTINCTION

Life has existed on Earth for nearly four billion years. Over that period, much of it has been wiped out five times in what are known as mass extinctions. The last one took place when a giant asteroid slammed into the planet 66 million years ago. Scientists now think we are in the middle of the "sixth extinction"—the first one caused by humans. Mammals—and all animals—are threatened. But conservationists are fighting to help. Here are six mammals brought back from the brink.

RODRIGUES FRUIT BAT

These flying mammals—also called Rodrigues flying foxes—originally lived on only one tiny group of islands in the middle of the Indian Ocean, about 1,000 miles (1,600 km) from Madagascar. There, the bats are essential for the health of their ecosystem because they eat fruit and spread the seeds in their droppings. But as a result of habitat loss, their population was decreasing, and conservationists worried that if there were a tropical cyclone, the bats could be wiped out completely. So now zoos across the world are home to captive bats—just in case.

SOUTHERN WHITE RHINOCEROS

The southern white rhino is the only species of rhino not listed as endangered today. Southern white rhinos live in South Africa, Zimbabwe, Namibia, and Kenya, where they have long been hunted for their horns. In the late 19th century, so few of them were left that they were thought to be extinct. But after more than 100 years of conservationists protecting southern white rhinos in certain areas of their habitat, about 20,000 of these animals are alive today.

HUMPBACK WHALE

These enormous ocean dwellers were hunted for their oil, meat, and the plates in their mouths called baleen from the 17th through 20th centuries. By the time commercial whale hunting ended, in 1985, more than 95 percent of humpbacks were gone from some populations. Though humpbacks still face threats from ship strikes and underwater noise, which can interfere with their communication, they are on the road to recovery: The International Union for Conservation of Nature (IUCN) no longer lists any humpback whale populations as endangered.

GOLDEN LION TAMARIN

This monkey with a mane like a lion is native to the Atlantic coastal rainforest of Brazil. These forests have been almost completely wiped out for logging, grazing cattle, and spreading urban areas—nearly wiping out the golden lion tamarin, too. By the 1970s, as few as 200 individuals were left. Conservationists stepped in to protect the remaining tamarins and to plant "corridors"—swaths of vegetation connecting the bits of habitat the monkeys had left. Now their numbers have risen to about 2,500.

MOUNTAIN GORILLA

Conflict between humans has destroyed the habitat in Africa's Congo Basin, the home of the mountain gorilla. Poachers hunt the gorillas that are left. About one-third of the remaining mountain gorillas live in Virunga National Park, a protected area since 1925. Despite many obstacles, such as illegal forest clearing in the park, Congolese scientists and conservationists have fought hard to protect mountain gorillas. And while it was once thought they would be extinct by the end of the 20th century, their numbers are slowly increasing today.

IBERIAN LYNX

Tufted-eared lynx have roamed the Iberian Peninsula, in southwestern Europe, for thousands of years. But two decades ago, there were fewer than 100 left in the wild. Hunting, habitat loss, and diseases that killed off their main prey—rabbits—had devastated the lynx population. Then conservationists began breeding lynx in captivity and releasing them into the wild. Now more than 600 of the spotted cats are stalking their way through the scrubland once again.

A WORLD OF MAMMALS

Mammals have evolved to live in nearly every habitat on Earth. From mountains to marshes, from prairies to poles, they have made their home on every continent—and throughout the ocean, too! This map shows where some well-known species can be found around the world.

Pacific Ocean

North America

Arctic Circle

Tropic of Cancer

Atlantic Ocean

Equator

South America

COYOTE

WOLVERINE

BOTTLENOSE DOLPHIN

BLUE WHALE

Southern

Antarctic Circle

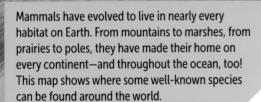
JAGUAR

TWO-TOED SLOTH

ELEPHANT SEAL

NARWHAL

POLAR BEAR

RED FOX

MOOSE

Arctic Ocean

SIBERIAN
TIGER

Europe

Asia

GIANT
PANDA

Pacific
Ocean

Africa

Indian
Ocean

Oceania

RED
KANGAROO

Tropic of Capricorn

0   2,000 miles

0   2,000 kilometers

Australia

KOALA

Ocean

Antarctica

AFRICAN
SAVANNA ELEPHANT

RETICULATED
GIRAFFE

AFRICAN LION

25

CHAPTER **TWO**

MEAT-EATING MAMMALS

CARNIVORES

ALL ABOUT CARNIVORES

They stalk through tall grass and lie in wait in tree branches. They attack using razor-sharp teeth and claws, powerful muscles, and honed senses. They are the carnivores.

While herbivores munch on plants, carnivores eat meat to survive. Some carnivores are large animals that hunt the biggest game on the planet; for example, lions are known to gather in groups to take down elephants. There are about 270 species of carnivores, all part of the mammal order called Carnivora. But not all members of Carnivora are strict meat-eaters; the kinkajou (p. 58), for example, dines on honey and fruit as well as on small mammals.

As meat-eaters, carnivores are at the top of the food chain. They play an important role in keeping their ecosystems healthy by keeping the populations of prey animals in check. If a predator disappears, prey animal populations can grow until there is no longer enough food or shelter in their environment. For this reason, scientists often look to predator populations to measure how healthy an ecosystem is.

AFRICAN CIVET

SCIENTIFIC NAME: *Civettictis civetta*

SIZE: Up to 3 feet (0.9 m) with a 2-foot (0.6-m) tail

WEIGHT: Up to 33 pounds (15 kg)

EATS: Insects, eggs, birds, reptiles, carrion, rodents, wild fruit

ORCA

SCIENTIFIC NAME: *Orcinus orca*

SIZE: Up to 32 feet (9.8 m)

WEIGHT: Up to 6 tons (5.4 t)

EATS: Fish, penguins, marine mammals

SOUTH AMERICAN SEA LION

SCIENTIFIC NAME: *Otaria flavescens*

SIZE: Up to 8 feet (2.4 m)

WEIGHT: Up to 770 pounds (350 kg)

EATS: Fish, squid, octopus

BOBCAT

SCIENTIFIC NAME: *Lynx rufus*

SIZE: Up to 3.4 feet (1 m) with a 7-inch (18-cm) tail

WEIGHT: Up to 30 pounds (14 kg)

EATS: Rabbits, birds, mice, squirrels, other smaller game

POLAR BEAR

SCIENTIFIC NAME: *Ursus maritimus*

SIZE: Up to 8 feet (2.4 m) with a 5-inch (13-cm) tail

WEIGHT: Up to 1,600 pounds (730 kg)

EATS: Seals

That's **Fact-tastic!**

Lions mostly live in **GRASSLAND HABITATS.** So why is the lion sometimes called the "king of the jungle"? It's because **"JUNGLE"** comes from the Sanskrit *jangala*, which means **"SPARSE"** or **"ARID."**

LION

ROOOOAAARRR! The call of the male African lion echoes across the savanna. This mighty carnivore has a head crowned by a thick mane of fur and, at more than 400 pounds (180 kg), weighs about as much as a ride-on lawn mower. But while a full-grown male lion is a hugely impressive sight, it's the females that are the main leaders and hunters.

Lions live in social groups called prides. A pride can have a few males and about a dozen females, all related to one another. Lionesses are faster and more agile than the males, so they do nearly all the hunting. They work together to capture prey—the smaller lionesses chase an antelope or zebra toward a spot where larger females wait in ambush. While the lionesses are hunting, the male lions guard the cubs. They're also in charge of protecting the pride.

A pride's lionesses often give birth around the same time. Mother lionesses keep their cubs in a secret spot for the first few weeks of their lives. They then bring them to the pride, where the cubs have lots of playmates to roll and pounce with. Raising cubs is a group effort, with all the females pitching in. They'll even nurse each other's cubs!

Lions once lived across most of Africa and even in parts of Asia and Europe. But today, they have disappeared from about 94 percent of their former range in sub-Saharan Africa. Another subspecies of lion, called Asiatic lions, has only one very small population that lives mostly in India's protected Gir National Park. Threats such as habitat loss and poaching put lions at risk today.

Like house cats, lions spend most of their time resting—up to 21 hours a day! Also like house cats, they like to lounge in funny positions, such as on their backs with all four feet in the air.

FACTS

SCIENTIFIC NAME *Panthera leo*

GROUP NAME Pride

SIZE Up to 6.5 feet (1.5 m) with a 3.3-foot (1-m) tail

WEIGHT Up to 420 pounds (191 kg)

EATS Antelope, zebras, hippos

Both **MALE** and **FEMALE** lions **ROAR.**

WILD CAT BREAKDOWN

CHEETAH VS. JAGUAR VS. LEOPARD

All three of these big cats are known for their distinctive spotted coats. So what makes each special?

JAGUAR

Jaguars appear similar to leopards, but if you look closely, you'll notice they have larger, rounded heads and shorter tails—as well as slightly different markings on their coats. Jaguars also inhabit a different part of the world than both leopards and cheetahs: They make their home in North, Central, and South America, often in tropical rainforests. Their strong limbs and large paws enable them to climb trees, slink along the forest floor, and even swim. They stalk their prey, ambush it, and then use powerful jaw muscles to pierce the animal's skull with their sharp teeth. Jaguars have the strongest bite of any big cat—twice as strong as a lion's!

CHEETAH

The cheetah is the world's fastest land animal, able to accelerate from zero to more than 60 miles an hour (97 km/h) in just three seconds. Cheetahs are so different from other big cats that they belong to their own genus, or group of related species. They are built for speed, with a small head and a long, lean body. Cheetahs have a flexible spine that allows their front legs to reach far forward as they run, allowing them to cover more ground. The cheetah's long tail acts as a rudder, helping the animal turn at high speed. And, unlike other cats, cheetahs cannot fully retract their claws, which give them extra traction, like the cleats on a runner's shoes. Cheetahs live mainly in eastern and southern Africa, with one population in Iran.

Leopards and jaguars **ROAR. CHEETAHS CAN'T.**

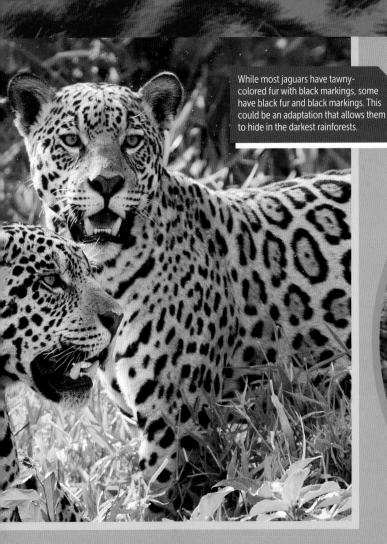

While most jaguars have tawny-colored fur with black markings, some have black fur and black markings. This could be an adaptation that allows them to hide in the darkest rainforests.

LEOPARD

The leopard is the smallest of the large cats. They are skilled hunters with muscular bodies that make them capable of incredible feats of strength. Leopards store their food up high in trees or hide it in dense brush to keep it safe from other predators. One leopard was spotted carrying a 220-pound (100-kg) juvenile giraffe—an animal about twice its own weight! They can even climb as high as 50 feet (15 m) up a tree with a fresh kill clenched in their jaws. Leopards are the most widespread big cats and are found in most of sub-Saharan Africa.

SPOT THE DIFFERENCE
WHICH COAT IS WHICH?

Leopard: Their spots are jagged black circles, called rosettes, that look a bit like—you guessed it—roses. A leopard's rosettes are small and close together.

Jaguar: Like leopards, jaguars also have rosettes. But theirs are large, often with a black spot in the center.

Cheetah: Cheetahs don't have rosettes at all. Instead, they sport solid black spots.

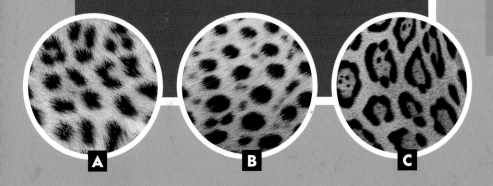

A

B

C

ANSWERS: A: leopard; B: cheetah; C: jaguar

That's Fact-tastic!

A bear's **DEEP WINTER SLEEP** is often called **HIBERNATION.** But scientists are currently debating whether bears are in fact true hibernators. Unlike with other hibernators, such as chipmunks, bears' **BODY TEMPERATURE DOES NOT DROP STEEPLY** during this time.

BROWN BEAR

It's wintertime. Snow falls softly on the ground. In a hollow under a fallen tree, an enormous brown bear snoozes. A brown bear can spend up to half the year in a deep sleeplike state. Its heart and metabolism slow down. It won't pee or poop for the entire winter, the only mammal on Earth to go that long without doing so.

Brown bears live across the world, from northern North America to Europe and Asia. They range in color from a light tan to nearly black. Alaska has a subspecies of brown bear called the Kodiak bear, which can grow to enormous size on a diet of salmon. In some parts of North America, brown bears are called grizzly bears because their fur is "grizzled," or tipped with white or tan.

Brown bears are not picky eaters. They will chow down on nearly anything they come across, from berries to carcasses left by other animals. Sometimes, they'll even hunt for creatures like rodents and young deer. In Alaska and in Russia, brown bears find their way to rivers to catch salmon as they swim upstream to spawn each summer. Usually, brown bears are solitary, but sometimes dozens of bears will gather together to grab the nutritious, fatty fish as they leap through the water.

That big appetite serves a purpose: Brown bears have to pack on as much weight as possible in the fall, sometimes gaining hundreds of pounds. Their bodies survive on this fat during the long winter while the bears are snoozing. Without this adaptation, these huge animals could not find enough food to fuel their big bodies during the time of year when food is scarce.

FACTS

SCIENTIFIC NAME *Ursus arctos*

GROUP NAME Sloth, sleuth

SIZE Up to 8 feet (2.4 m)

WEIGHT Up to 700 pounds (318 kg)

EATS Anything from roots to insects to salmon

Female bears don't merely **SURVIVE** the **WINTER**—they actually **GIVE BIRTH** during the coldest part of the year! Usually, **TWO CUBS** are **BORN** at once.

35

SIBERIAN TIGER

FACTS

SCIENTIFIC NAME *Panthera tigris altaica*

GROUP NAME Streak, ambush

SIZE 11 feet (3.4 m)

WEIGHT About 660 pounds (300 kg)

EATS Wild boar, sika deer, elk

Enormous but nearly silent, the Siberian tiger prowls through the northern forests of Russia, China, and North Korea. Some say it is the largest wild cat in the world. This powerful predator hunts at night, using stealth to sneak up on large prey such as elk and wild boar. After a quick pounce and a fatal bite, the hunter has its dinner.

Siberian tigers, sometimes called Amur tigers, weigh in at about 660 pounds (300 kg)—heavier than a baby grand piano. Like their cousins, the Bengal tigers, Siberians have striped fur that acts as camouflage, helping them blend into tall grass and branches. To help survive in the snowy northern regions where temperatures can dip to minus 4°F (-20°C), the Siberian grows a thick, fluffy coat in the winter.

Tigers are solitary creatures that require vast areas of land to thrive: A single male tiger's habitat can cover 772 square miles (2,000 sq km)! That's because food is scarce in the Siberian tiger's remote home, and the tigers often must travel far to find a meal. But even though they live alone, tigers still communicate with each other. They mark their territory with their scent to keep rivals away, and they also use low-frequency sound—too low for human ears to detect—to call to each other.

A century ago, Siberian tigers could be found across Russia and China from the Caspian Sea to the Pacific Ocean. By 1940, there were just a few dozen of them left in the wild. Their habitat has disappeared due to illegal logging in the Russian Far East. And poachers hunt the tigers as trophies and for use in traditional medicine. But their numbers have recovered a bit: Today, about 500 Siberian tigers live in the wild.

Siberian tigers' **TONGUES** are **SO ROUGH** they can **LOOSEN MEAT** from **BONE.**

That's
Fact-tastic!

Tigers **DON'T** need to **EAT EVERY DAY.** In the wild, they often kill prey a few times a week and then **GORGE** on up to **60 POUNDS** (27 kg) of **MEAT** in a single sitting.

ANIMAL WEAPONS

Carnivores can hunt in the frozen polar regions or stalk prey across the desert. They can chase down prey during the light of day or wait until the sun sinks below the horizon to stage their attack. Carnivorous mammals take many forms. But most have similar adaptations to help them hunt.

Adaptations are physical features or behaviors that help a living thing survive. Because carnivores all must find, attack, and eat prey, they share many adaptations, such as the keen senses they use to hunt. Most rely on a strong sense of vision and have eyes located in the front of their head. That means that the area each eye sees overlaps, allowing a predator to sense how far away the prey is and how fast it's moving. This is called binocular vision, and humans have it, too. Predators usually have sensitive hearing, as well. Many predatory mammals, such as foxes (p. 46), can swivel their ears around. This helps them pinpoint the direction a sound is coming from, allowing them to track prey with great precision. Many predators also have a powerful sense of smell. Black bears, for example, can sniff out food from miles away.

RED FOX

BALD EAGLE

NOT-SO-FURRY
CARNIVORES

Not all meat-eaters belong to the mammal order Carnivora. Predatory birds, such as eagles, use sharp vision to hunt prey from above and long talons to grab it. Reptiles such as chameleons use their long tongues to snag insects. And many spiders use venom to paralyze their prey.

Wolverines have strong teeth and powerful jaws.

GRIZZLY BEAR CLAWS

WOLVERINE

CHEETAH

Predators use **CAMOUFLAGE** to **SNEAK UP** on their prey without being seen.

Once predatory mammals track down their prey, they must kill and eat it. Many predators have either sharp teeth, piercing claws, or powerful jaws—and some have all three! Most predators have multiple kinds of teeth. There are incisors in the front, used to cut food. Pointed canine teeth on the sides can kill by piercing an animal's hide and can also tear off food for eating. Molars in the back are flat, used for grinding up food. Many predators snap their teeth closed with powerful jaws. A wolverine, for example, has jaws strong enough to chomp through bone! Sharp claws can be powerful weapons, too. Most big cats, such as lions and tigers, can pull in their claws when running to keep them sharp. They push out their claws when needed to rip and tear. How ferocious!

That's
Fact-tastic!

Though coyotes **PREFER** to be on **LAND,** they are **EXCELLENT SWIMMERS.** They will swim to hunt aquatic animals such as **FROGS** and **FISH.** Coyotes have even been known to use their swimming skills to make a new home on islands.

COYOTE

A chorus of howls fills the night air. It's a pack of coyotes preparing to begin the hunt. Coyotes howl to gather the pack together and to keep other packs in the area out of their territory. Coyotes once lived only in the prairies and deserts of western North America. But today, their howls can be heard across much of the continent.

Coyotes appear as clever characters in the tales of many North American Indigenous groups. And these creatures deserve the reputation: They are intelligent animals that use keen senses of sight, smell, and hearing to find food. Coyotes hunt small mammals such as mice and rabbits, but they will make a meal out of just about anything they can find, from snakes to insects to fruit, grass, and even garbage. This adaptability has helped coyotes thrive in new habitats. Today, they can even be found prowling the streets of big cities such as Los Angeles and New York!

Some of the time, coyotes hunt alone. Their speed—up to 40 miles an hour (65 km/h)—makes them formidable hunters. But in the fall and winter, they'll team up in packs for even more predator power.

Springtime is when coyote pups are born. Females give birth in dens often hidden under fallen trees. Though they can dig their own dens, savvy coyotes prefer to take over and enlarge the burrows of animals such as foxes or skunks. After the pups are born, both coyote parents pitch in to help raise them. As the pups grow to adulthood, the females will usually stay with the parents. The males will leave their home territory and use their coyote cleverness to survive on their own.

FACTS

SCIENTIFIC NAME *Canis latrans*

GROUP NAME Pack

SIZE Up to 37 inches (94 cm) with a 16-inch (41-cm) tail

WEIGHT Up to 50 pounds (23 kg)

EATS Anything from small mammals to insects to plants

Coyotes are known for **HOWLING AT THE MOON.** But they don't really—they just happen to **HUNT AT NIGHT** and **HOWL TO COMMUNICATE** with other coyotes.

GRAY WOLF

FACTS

SCIENTIFIC NAME *Canis lupus*

GROUP NAME Pack

SIZE Up to 5.25 feet (1.6 m) with a 20-inch (50-cm) tail

WEIGHT Up to 175 pounds (79 kg)

EATS Deer, elk, moose, fish, birds, lizards, fruit

A **wolf prances toward another pack member, ears** pointed forward and tail wagging. It bows low, its upper body touching the ground and rump held high. It wants to play! The two wolves roll and tumble on the ground. If this behavior sounds familiar, it's because the gray wolf is a close relative of the domestic dog.

Gray wolves and dogs share an ancestor that lived sometime between 40,000 and 20,000 years ago. While the ancestor of today's dogs began to form a close partnership with humans, the ancestor of modern wolves stayed wild. Today, gray wolves roam parts of the northwestern United States, parts of Eurasia, and parts of North Africa. They can thrive in many kinds of habitats, from tundra to forests to deserts.

Wolves live in packs that can have just a few or more than 15 members. Wolves usually mate for life, and a pack is made up of parents and their offspring. The pack will hunt together to bring down large prey such as deer, elk, and moose. To work as a team, wolves use a complex system of communication. Besides body language, they make many sounds, such as barking, whimpering, growling, and howling. A howl can tell other wolves to watch out for a predator or indicate the location of prey. Every day, all the wolves in a pack will howl together—maybe as a way to strengthen their pack bond.

In North America, wolves once lived across two-thirds of the continent. Then they were hunted by European settlers until they disappeared from most of their range. As a result of strong conservation efforts, the numbers of gray wolves are on the rise again.

A WOLF'S HOWL can be HEARD 10 MILES (16 km) AWAY.

That's Fact-tastic!

Though many people think of **WOLVES** as **DANGEROUS**, **HUMANS** are a much **BIGGER DANGER** to wolves than wolves are to humans. Although **WOLVES** will **KILL LIVESTOCK** animals such as **COWS** if they're **HUNGRY**, they **RARELY ATTACK PEOPLE.** A person has a greater chance of being killed by a bee sting or struck by lightning than of being injured by a wolf.

43

SECRETS OF HUNTERS

BADGER AND COYOTE

There are no easy meals for the carnivores of the mammal world. Carnivores can survive only by targeting and taking down other animals—a way of living that requires smarts, savvy, and strategy. Here are the tactics carnivores use to find the food they need.

JACKAL

SCAVENGING

Hunting is hard work. So some meat-eaters simply choose not to. While jackals can hunt small animals for themselves, they instead often eat the remains of another hunter's dinner. In Africa, jackals commonly help themselves to what's left after a big cat such as a lion or leopard has eaten. Sometimes, jackals will even work together to grab a bite from the hunter. That's a lot of risk for some leftovers!

PACK HUNTING

There's only one way an animal the size of a domestic dog can tackle a 440-pound (200-kg) wildebeest: teamwork. African wild dogs live in packs of up to 20. These groups are so tight-knit that they have even been known to assist weak members of the pack by sharing food. When it's time to hunt, the dogs use different strategies for different prey: For instance, a few dogs might charge a herd of wildebeest to flush out a slow individual, then the rest go in for the kill.

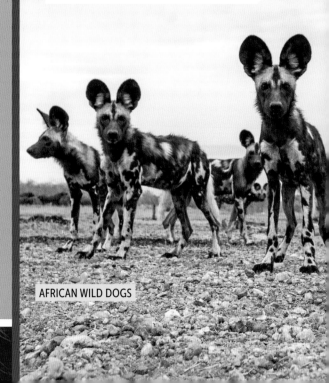
AFRICAN WILD DOGS

CLOUDED LEOPARD

AMBUSH

Like most wild cats, clouded leopards use stealth to attack their prey. Clouded leopards thrive in the treetops, where they can leap from branch to branch with ease, climb head-first down from treetops, and even hang from branches by their hind feet. They'll wait in the trees, still and quiet, until prey comes along on the ground below. Then they'll drop down in a surprise attack.

COOPERATIVE HUNTING

Sometimes, it's not just animals within a group or pack that use teamwork to catch their dinner. Animals of two different species will occasionally cooperate for the sake of survival, too. In North America, coyotes and badgers have been spotted hunting together. A coyote will sometimes chase a prairie dog into an underground burrow, where the badger can dig it out. Or the badger will dig into a squirrel den, flushing out a ground squirrel that the coyote then chases down.

CHEETAH

PURSUIT

It's the fastest land animal for a reason. Unlike most other cats, the cheetah doesn't hide and wait for its prey to come close enough to pounce. Instead, it uses its incredible speed to chase down its meals. Cheetahs hunt in the daytime, using their keen vision to scan the grassland for prey. When a cheetah finds the right target, it takes off in a blazing-fast sprint, using both its speed and agility to overtake its prey. This strategy uses up so much energy that cheetah hunts usually last less than a minute.

That's Fact-tastic!

When red foxes **POUNCE** on **PREY HIDING UNDER** the **SNOW,** they almost always **LEAP** in a **NORTHEASTERLY DIRECTION.** Scientists think the foxes could be **ALIGNING** their **LEAPS** with **EARTH'S MAGNETIC FIELD,** which gives them incredible accuracy. **OTHER ANIMALS** that can **SENSE** Earth's **MAGNETIC FIELD** include sharks, ants, and turtles.

RED FOX

The red fox crouches on the snow, concentrating on something beneath the frozen surface. It tilts its head from side to side, listening for something far too quiet for humans to hear—then it springs. Leaping high into the air, it dives headfirst into the powder—and emerges with a mouse clamped between its teeth. Success!

This unusual technique is just one of the ways foxes find food. These animals seek out small prey like rodents, rabbits, and birds. But foxes are resourceful, and they'll also dine on fruit, vegetables, frogs, and worms. That helps them survive in a wide range of places. Foxes live on every continent except South America and Antarctica. They shelter in dens, which they use as a cozy place to sleep, a pantry to store food, and a nursery to raise their pups. Foxes build multiple exits into their burrows so that they can escape quickly if threatened.

Foxes are part of the dog family, related to wolves and jackals. But in some ways, they're more like cats than dogs. Unless they are raising pups, foxes are solitary animals. They have sensitive whiskers. They walk on their toes, giving them a stealthy, silent way of moving. And, like cats, they have vertical pupils that help them see in dim light. A related species, the gray fox, can even climb trees!

Foxes are known to be shy but curious creatures. They've been spotted playing with other animals, such as dogs, that they meet. They've even been filmed stealing balls from golf courses! Humans have long been fascinated with foxes, too. In 2011, it was announced that researchers in Jordan discovered the 16,500-year-old grave of a man buried alongside a fox.

FACTS

SCIENTIFIC NAME *Vulpes vulpes*

GROUP NAME Skulk

SIZE Up to 34 inches (86 cm) with a 22-inch (56-cm) tail

WEIGHT Up to 24 pounds (11 kg)

EATS Small mammals, birds, fruit, vegetables, insects

Foxes can make **40 DIFFERENT SOUNDS.**

SPOTTED HYENA

FACTS

SCIENTIFIC NAME *Crocuta crocuta*

GROUP NAME Clan

SIZE Up to 5 feet (1.5 m)

WEIGHT Up to 190 pounds (86 kg)

EATS Everything from ostrich eggs to full-grown buffalo

AARDWOLF

The **SMALLEST MEMBER** of the **HYENA FAMILY**, the **AARDWOLF, EATS** only **TERMITES.**

Hyenas have a reputation for lacking intelligence. But that's far from the truth. These top predators are misunderstood: They're actually highly intelligent hunters. Though hyenas look similar to dogs, they aren't even related to dogs. In fact, hyenas are more closely related to cats! There are four species of hyena—spotted, striped, brown, and the aardwolf. Spotted hyenas are the largest, standing 2.6 feet (81 cm) at the shoulder. They have large heads; thick, muscular necks; and extremely powerful jaws. The spotted hyena has one of the strongest bites of any mammal on Earth.

Spotted hyenas live in large, complex groups called clans that can include more than 100 animals. Hyenas not only use their smarts for hunting, they also keep track of social bonds among their many clan-mates and remember the relationships those animals have with one another. Spotted hyena clans are matriarchal, or ruled by females, which are usually larger and more aggressive than the males. The lowest-ranking female hyena in the clan ranks higher than its highest-ranking male. If a male hyena makes a kill on his own, he has to hurry and eat before a female comes along and steals it from him!

Though they are sometimes depicted as scavengers that merely eat the kills of other animals, hyenas hunt for most of their meals. They can hunt alone or in groups. Alone, they often go for smaller prey such as rabbits, foxes, jackals, and fish. In groups, hyenas can take down prey many times their size, such as buffalo, wildebeest, and zebras. They eat nearly all of what they kill, down to its skin, hooves, bones, and teeth.

That's Fact-tastic!

Hyenas have a **REPUTATION** as **MEAL-STEALING THIEVES.** But they are also **EXCELLENT HUNTERS.** In fact, when **LIONS** and **HYENAS** are spotted **SHARING** an animal **CARCASS,** it's usually the **HYENAS** that **MADE** the **KILL.**

PACK LIFE

AFRICAN LIONS

Tigers and wolverines stalk their territories alone. But many mammals live and hunt in groups. Why do two of the most well-known pack hunters—wolves and lions—choose to team up?

Wolves and lions are fierce hunters. They are perfectly capable of hunting alone, chasing down and eating smaller prey like rabbits, mice, and birds. A lioness can even take down animals as large as wildebeest without assistance! But these apex predators—the top of their food chains—often hunt for large animals: Wolves prey on elk, caribou, and moose. Lions hunt zebras, rhinos, and, rarely, hippos. And bringing down large animals is easier in a group.

Lionesses come together in hunting parties. They will chase their prey at high speeds, surrounding it. Then they leap, jumping on the backs of large animals and using their

ANIMAL BABYSITTERS

Pack life doesn't just help animals when they're hunting. Raising little wolves and lions is a big job that's easier in a group. A wolf mother will stay in the den, nursing her young, and she relies on other members of the pack to bring back food for her to eat. Likewise, every lioness in the pride pitches in to raise the cubs. Females even give birth around the same time and often nurse each other's babies.

AFRICAN LIONS

LIONS are the ONLY WILD CATS that LIVE in GROUPS.

WOLVES

GRAY WOLVES

powerful jaws to deliver a fatal bite to the neck. Rarely, male lions will join the hunting party to help bring down a large animal like an elephant or water buffalo. Group hunting also helps lions prey on herd animals such as antelope and zebras. Because they live in herds, these animals have hundreds of eyes constantly watching out for danger, making it tough for a predator to sneak up without being noticed. But by hunting as a group, several lions can close in on their prey from several directions at once, encircling it so that it has nowhere to run.

A wolf pack is a complex social group. Each pack is led by an alpha male and alpha female that make all the decisions and are the parents to all the pups. The rest of the pack has a strict hierarchy, or order. It goes all the way from the beta wolf, or second-in-command (who helps keep the peace and acts as a babysitter to the pups), to the omega, or the lowest-ranking wolf in the pack. Wolves hunt together, surrounding prey and knocking it to the ground. But they don't eat together—the alpha male dines before any other wolf has a bite. The structure of a wolf pack changes over time. A wolf lower down in the pecking order may challenge the alpha. If the alpha loses, the challenger will become the new pack leader.

WOLVERINE

FACTS

SCIENTIFIC NAME *Gulo gulo*

GROUP NAME Pack, gang, mob

SIZE Up to 34 inches (86 cm) with a 10-inch (25-cm) tail

WEIGHT Up to 40 pounds (18 kg)

EATS Rabbits, caribou, moose, elk, carrion

Wolverines are **SMART** enough to **STEAL BAIT** out of **TRAPS** set by **SCIENTISTS** who are trying to **CAPTURE** the animals, **OUTFIT** them with **TRACKING COLLARS**, and then release them back into the wild.

The clawed comic book character gets its name from this animal for a reason: Wolverines are some of the toughest mammals on the planet. Equipped with long, slicing claws and an attitude to match, wolverines prowl the taiga and tundra of northern Europe, Asia, and North America.

Food is often scarce in these snow-covered areas, especially during winter. Wolverines survive by being willing to take on nearly any creature they come across. They routinely hunt smaller prey such as rabbits and rodents but also regularly attack animals much larger than they are, such as caribou. They'll also happily eat the carcasses of animals such as elk and deer.

Wolverines look like small, furry bears, but they are actually a type of weasel. Though the largest wolverines weigh just 40 pounds (18 kg)—about as much as a medium-size dog—they have no problem facing off with wolves or bears if a meal is on the line. These creatures roam vast distances in search of their next meal, traveling up to 15 miles (24 km) in a single day. To locate food, they use their superpowered sense of smell: A wolverine's nose is so sensitive it can sniff out prey hiding six feet (1.8 m) under the snow, allowing it to find the carcasses of animals killed in avalanches. When it finds its next meal, it uses teeth and jaws so powerful that they can crush bones. These animals even have specialized sideways teeth that can tear through frozen carcasses. Whatever they can't finish, they'll save for later by burying it in the snow, using the snow like a refrigerator! Wolverines were once hunted for their thick, frost-resistant fur, which was used to line parkas. Today, conservationists are fighting to protect these iconic animals.

That's Fact-tastic!

The wolverine's **SCIENTIFIC NAME** means **"GLUTTON"**—a **WORD** for **SOMEONE** who **EATS TOO MUCH.** True to their name, wolverines **ALWAYS** seem to be **HUNGRY:** Shortly after **CHOWING DOWN** on one **MEAL,** they'll head off in **SEARCH** of the **NEXT.**

THE WEASEL FAMILY

The ferocious wolverine (p. 52) is the largest member of the weasel family. But its cousins—though smaller in size—are no less fearsome. These cunning predators live in most parts of the world. The weasel family, called the mustelids, is one of the oldest groups of carnivores on Earth. They have been roaming the planet for as long as 30 million years.

FISHER

Sometimes called "fisher cats," fishers aren't cats at all. Instead, they are members of the weasel family that live in Canada and small areas of the United States. Fishers are carnivores that eat creatures such as rabbits and hares. They also eat porcupines—one of the few mammals that does. To dine on this prickly prey, fishers stage an aggressive attack, biting at any part of the porcupine not covered by quills.

NORTH AMERICAN RIVER OTTER

This sleek creature is perfectly at home both in the water and on land. River otters live in burrows on the edge of rivers, using a network of tunnels to enter and exit. At night, they head to the water, where they use webbed feet and water-repellent fur to hunt comfortably underwater. They will eat whatever they can find, from fish to turtles to frogs. On land, they've been known to slide down snowy or muddy hills—and they seem to do it just for fun!

STOAT

Stoats bound across grasslands and woodlands in northern Europe, Asia, and North America. These long-bodied predators are perfectly adapted for diving into burrows after rodents and small rabbits, which they kill instantly with a bite to the back of the skull. Stoats hunt strategically, searching an area in a zigzag pattern so they don't overlook a potential meal. In the winter, when their coats turn white, they are sometimes called ermine.

AMERICAN MARTEN

These forest dwellers use semi-retractable claws a bit like a cat's to climb trees and leap from branch to branch. They have scent glands they use to mark their trails through the treetops, communicating their location to other martens. Martens spend much of their time investigating every crack and crevice for food. They'll eat anything from mice and squirrels to eggs, berries, and nuts. In the winter, they use their furry feet to tunnel through the snow in search of a meal.

ZORILLA

It resembles a skunk, but this weasel is a separate species that lives only in Africa. It's called a zorilla, striped polecat, or African skunk. Although skunks are mostly gentle creatures, zorillas can be aggressive. They have sharp teeth and claws that they use to hunt for snakes, birds, small rodents, and insects. And, like a skunk, the zorilla has a powerful defense: a stinky spray that it unleashes from glands under its tail.

LEAST WEASEL

No more than seven inches (18 cm) long, including their tail, least weasels are tiny but mighty carnivores. They use their small size to their advantage, darting into holes to snap up mice and voles with razor-sharp teeth. According to legends of the Blackfeet people, an Indigenous group from the Great Plains area of the United States, the least weasel is the bravest of all animals.

That's
Fact-tastic!

FENNEC FOXES use their
UNUSUALLY LARGE EARS
to SENSE PREY moving
underneath the sand. When
they FIND a RODENT or
LIZARD, they will DIG quickly
with all four FEET to
UNCOVER their MEAL,
then GOBBLE
IT DOWN.

FENNEC FOX

The smallest fox in the world has ears so enormous they look like satellite dishes. But they're more than just adorable: The fennec fox's outsize ears—the largest for their body size of any member of the canine family—help them survive in their hot home.

Fennec foxes live in the Sahara, a desert in Africa where temperatures sometimes top 122°F (50°C). Survival in this extreme environment is no easy feat. The fox's big ears give off body heat, helping the animal keep cool. Fennec foxes also have furry paws that protect their feet from the hot ground. They spend the day, when temperatures are at their hottest, burrowed underground in sand dunes. A thick, light-colored coat reflects sunlight during the day—and also keeps the fox warm when desert temperatures plummet at night.

Fennec foxes are social creatures that live in small family groups. Sometimes, multiple families will even share a single den. At dusk, fennec foxes come out of these underground homes to search for food. They use their large ears to help them find scurrying prey. Like their cousin, the red fox, they are omnivores—animals that eat both plants and animals. They feast on everything from lizards to fruits, roots, and eggs. They drink almost no water, instead getting nearly all the moisture they need from the plants they eat—a nifty trick in a dry environment!

Fennec foxes form deep bonds. When they find a mate, the relationship is for life. Fennec foxes usually give birth to one litter of babies, called kits, each year. When the babies are born, the female fox cares for them in the burrow, while the male fox brings food for the mother and babies.

FACTS

SCIENTIFIC NAME *Vulpes zerda*

GROUP NAME Skulk, leash

SIZE Up to 16 inches (41 cm) with a tail up to 12 inches (31 cm) long

WEIGHT Up to 3.3 pounds (1.5 kg)

EATS Rodents, eggs, reptiles, plants, insects

The **FENNEC FOX** is a **MEMBER** of the **CANINE FAMILY,** which also includes wolves, coyotes, foxes, jackals, dingoes, and domestic dogs.

KINKAJOU

FACTS

SCIENTIFIC NAME *Potos flavus*

GROUP NAME Troop, convergence

SIZE Up to 22 inches (56 cm) with a tail up to 22 inches (56 cm) long

WEIGHT Up to 7 pounds (3 kg)

EATS Nectar, honey, fruit, small mammals

A **furry creature hangs by its tail from a branch in a** South American rainforest. It's munching on fruit—one of its favorite foods. Kinkajous have quite the sweet tooth, and they especially enjoy using their long tongues to slurp up flower nectar and honey. But this furry tree dweller is actually a carnivore, related to raccoons. It has canine teeth and sometimes dines on small mammals.

Kinkajous look a bit like primates. And, like some primates, they have a special tail called a prehensile tail that they can use to grip tree branches. Kinkajous and an animal called a binturong (p. 248) are the only two carnivores that have prehensile tails. Kinkajous don't just use this tail to hold on to branches. They also use it to grab food and even snuggle up underneath it while sleeping.

The forest is full of predators like jaguars and harpy eagles. Kinkajous venture out only at night and make sure to hide away in a tree hollow or crook before sunrise, when most predators are on the prowl. If it does get chased by an attacker, the kinkajou deploys a secret weapon: It can rotate its hind ankles to turn its feet around, giving it the ability to climb down a tree's trunk headfirst. That allows the kinkajou to make a speedy escape!

Kinkajous live nearly their whole lives in the treetops. And as they move from tree to tree, they play a major role in keeping their forest homes healthy. Just like bees and butterflies, kinkajous are pollinators. When they drink nectar, pollen from one flower sticks to their faces and is carried to the next flower. That helps the plants reproduce, so there will be flowers and fruit for kinkajous to feast on the following year.

The kinkajou's **THICK COAT PROTECTS** it from **BEE STINGS** while it **SEARCHES** for **HONEY.**

That's **Fact-tastic!**

NEWBORN KINKAJOUS are so HELPLESS they CAN'T even SEE. But they grow up quickly. By the END of their SECOND MONTH of life, young kinkajous are so AGILE they can HANG UPSIDE DOWN from their TAILS!

CARNIVORES
IN YOUR BACKYARD

You don't have to travel all the way to the jungle or forest to see carnivores in the wild. You can find some sharp-toothed hunters living right under your nose!

BADGER

Their fluffy faces and waddling way of walking might be cute, but make no mistake: Badgers are ferocious carnivores. They use their webbed front feet and shovel-shaped back claws to dig into the burrows of ground squirrels and other small animals, and then tear their prey apart with their sharp teeth. Often, they use their digging skills to bury food for later. A biologist in Utah, U.S.A., once witnessed a badger bury an entire cow carcass!

STRIPED SKUNK

Oh no! When you spot that black-and-white-striped coat, you know to back off. Striped skunks, which are widespread across North America, are infamous for their ability to spray a smelly blast at oncoming attackers. Although they are omnivores that eat both plants and animals, skunks are part of the Carnivora order of mammals. They hunt insects, grubs, and even rats, rabbits, and other small mammals.

MONGOOSE

This family of sleek, furry critters lives mostly in Africa, where they dwell in trees or underground burrows. They eat small mammals, birds, and reptiles, and they have an unusual way of eating eggs. Some mongoose species have been observed standing with their back to a rock, and then throwing an egg between their legs and against the rock to crack the shell. Many mongoose species also hunt venomous snakes. Though they are sometimes bitten, they are immune to snake venom.

MOUNTAIN LION

Also known as the cougar, puma, panther, or catamount, this big cat lives across the Americas, making its home in all kinds of environments, from deserts to wetlands. Mountain lions mostly stalk and kill deer, but they will eat smaller creatures when they have to. They require huge territories of about 100 square miles (260 sq km) to survive. Sometimes, that puts them in close contact with people. In years of monitoring mountain lions in the Santa Monica Mountains around Los Angeles, for example, scientists have observed more than 75 of the big cats!

WHITE-NOSED COATI

It looks a bit like a raccoon with a long nose. But this critter is a coati, a carnivore that inhabits parts of North and South America. Coatis sleep at night, then spend their days traveling around in packs of about two dozen or more, looking for food. They use their long, flexible noses to poke underneath rocks and into piles of leaves to search for insects, fruit, rodents, lizards, and snakes.

That's
Fact-tastic!

Though it's **CALLED** a snow
"LEOPARD" and has a **SPOTTED
COAT**, this cat **BELONGS** to a
DIFFERENT FAMILY than the
leopard. In fact, snow leopards are
**MORE CLOSELY RELATED TO
TIGERS.** But unlike tigers and most
other big cats, **SNOW LEOPARDS
CAN'T ROAR.** Instead, they
GROWL, HISS, and **SPIT.**

SNOW LEOPARD

The snow leopard appears, stalking across a steep, rocky mountaintop in the Himalaya. It moves on nearly silent paws and is so elusive it's almost never spotted in the wild. It's no wonder this graceful cat is often referred to as the "ghost of the mountains."

Snow leopards live high in the mountain ranges of Central Asia. But their secretive natures and far-flung habitat make them mysterious creatures. In local folklore, they are sometimes described as mountain spirits that can change their shape at will. For scientists, the snow leopard's lifestyle makes this cat difficult to study.

These cats may live in an extreme environment, but they are well adapted to it. They have dense fur that covers even the bottoms of their huge feet, giving them great grip on snow and extra cushion for walking, climbing, and jumping. They have large noses that warm chilly air on its way to their lungs. And their long, thick tail—sometimes as long as their body—helps them balance when navigating the steep cliffs and rocks of their home. When the temperature dips, snow leopards use their tail like a furry blanket, wrapping it around their body for extra warmth.

Snow leopards live where food is scarce. To survive, they have to be fierce hunters. They eat marmots, birds, and small rodents but are also capable of killing large animals such as blue sheep and ibex. Snow leopards can bring down prey up to three times their own weight! Because food is hard to come by where they live, snow leopards need huge ranges to survive. Though they roam across 12 countries, there are probably no more than a few thousand of them in the wild.

FACTS

SCIENTIFIC NAME *Panthera uncia*

GROUP NAME None

SIZE Up to 4.25 feet (1.3 m) with a tail up to 3.25 feet (1 m) long

WEIGHT Up to 121 pounds (55 kg)

EATS Birds, rodents, blue sheep, ibex

These cats can **LEAP SIX TIMES** their **BODY LENGTH.**

PYGMY SHREW

FACTS

SCIENTIFIC NAME *Sorex minutus*

GROUP NAME None

SIZE Up to 2.3 inches (6 cm) with a tail up to 1.8 inches (4.5 cm) long

WEIGHT Up to 0.2 ounce (6 g)

EATS Insects

The petite pygmy shrew weighs a bit more than a penny. But it eats 125 percent of its body weight daily. That's like a seven-year-old kid chowing down on 25 pizzas each day!

This hungry hunter is Ireland's smallest mammal. Once thought to be a native animal of Ireland, genetic and fossil data show that it actually arrived there within the past few thousand years, probably when humans accidentally brought it from Britain.

Pygmy shrews spend nearly every moment foraging for food. To stay alive, they must constantly capture and eat prey. If they go longer than about two hours without food, they will die. Extremely aggressive for their size, they speed through their territories, looking for spiders, woodlice, and other insects to devour. They are not afraid to face off against other pygmy shrews when competing for territory. When fighting or threatened, they make a "chit" sound.

Experts think the shrews do not dig their own burrows but instead take over the burrows of other animals to raise their young. Within its short lifespan—only about a year—a pygmy shrew might have just one or two litters of about six young. But because pygmy shrews are extremely shy, much about their lifestyles is unknown.

Pygmy shrews are **ACTIVE BOTH** during the **DAY** and at **NIGHT**.

That's Fact-tastic!

Experts think pygmy shrews may need to **EAT** more than **250 INSECTS EACH DAY.** That makes them **FIERCE PREDATORS,** despite their tiny size!

EXTINCT CARNIVORES

Today's lions and tigers might seem fierce—until you compare them with some of the meat-eaters that lived long ago. These were mammals you wouldn't want to mess with.

CAVE BEAR

In 2011, scientists reanalyzed the fossil of a short-faced bear that had been discovered in 1935 and were shocked at what they found. They estimated that the living creature would have weighed 3,500 pounds (1,600 kg) and stood at least 11 feet (3.4 m) tall when on its hind legs. This massive mammal roamed South America until just about 500,000 years ago. And, unlike its modern, omnivorous relatives, it ate only meat. Experts think it might have made a meal out of the giant Ice Age mammals that also lived at the time, such as giant sloths.

PACHYCROCUTA

At the same time prehistoric humans were making their way around the globe, so was a hyena as heavy as a lion. That was *Pachycrocuta brevirostris*. The largest hyena that ever lived, it was about as tall as today's spotted hyenas but three times heavier, making it one bulky beast. Like a modern hyena's, *Pachycrocuta*'s tough teeth would have made it capable of crunching through bone. Tooth marks on fossilized bone show that this mega hyena dined on elephant carcasses—and human ones, too.

ANDREWSARCHUS

It was perhaps the largest predatory mammal to ever exist. A relative of the modern hippo, *Andrewsarchus* lived about 45 million years ago and is known from only a single, nearly three-foot (1-m)-long skull discovered in Mongolia in 1923. Scientists have never found fossils of the animal's body, but, judging from its head, *Andrewsarchus* was about six feet (1.8 m) high at the shoulder and 12 feet (3.6 m) long.

DIRE WOLF

This creature sometimes makes an appearance in fantasy TV. But it's no invention: The dire wolf was a real-life animal. The dire wolf, or *Canis dirus,* lived from about 125,000 to 10,000 years ago across much of the Americas. It was a relative of today's gray wolf and looked similar to a modern wolf, just bigger. Dire wolves weighed about 130 pounds (60 kg), with stocky proportions and big teeth—all the better to eat horses, bison, and maybe even mammoths.

SMILODON

Just 10,000 years ago, the saber-toothed cat *Smilodon fatalis* prowled North America. Experts are divided over whether *Smilodon* slunk through forests, stalking tapirs and deer, or chased down bison and horses on grasslands. But one thing's for sure: This was one killer cat. *Smilodon* clocked in at up to 600 pounds (270 kg) and sported seven-inch (18-cm)-long canine teeth.

CHAPTER **THREE**

HOOFED MAMMALS

UNGULATES

ALL ABOUT UNGULATES

They move across savannas and grasslands around the world. Most are built for speed, with long legs that help them run far and fast. Amazingly, they do this running on toes that evolved over time to become tipped in hornlike tissue called hooves. These creatures are the ungulates, or hoofed mammals.

There are two groups of ungulates alive today. The Artiodactyla ("even-toed") order includes more than 100 species that walk on two toes, including sheep, goats, camels, pigs, and antelope. The Perissodactyla ("odd-toed") order has only 17 living species. Some, such as rhinos and tapirs, walk on three toes. Others, such as horses, walk on one toe. The ancestor of the Artiodactyla and the Perissodactyla was also the ancestor of some animals that don't have hooves at all, such as elephants, whales, and dolphins.

Almost all ungulates are herbivores, or strict plant-eaters, like deer. Many have large, grooved molar teeth that they use for chewing up tough grasses and leaves. To get as much nutrition as possible from their vegetarian diet, some ungulates—like cows—are ruminants, meaning they chew their food, swallow it, then bring it back up to chew it again. This behavior might sound gross, but it allows animals with big bodies that need a lot of energy to survive on a diet of plants.

LESSER MOUSE-DEER

SCIENTIFIC NAME: *Tragulus kanchil*

SIZE: About 1.5 feet (0.5 m)

WEIGHT: About 5 pounds (2.3 kg)

EATS: Grass, leaves, fallen fruits, seeds

HARTEBEEST

SCIENTIFIC NAME: *Alcelaphus buselaphus*

SIZE: Up to 8 feet (2.4 m)

WEIGHT: Up to 440 pounds (200 kg)

EATS: Grass

DONKEY

SCIENTIFIC NAME: *Equus asinus*

SIZE: About 4 feet (1.2 m) tall

WEIGHT: About 550 pounds (250 kg)

EATS: Straw, hay, grass

COLLARED PECCARY

SCIENTIFIC NAME: *Pecari tajacu*

SIZE: About 3 to 4 feet (0.9–1.2 m)

WEIGHT: Up to 55 pounds (25 kg)

EATS: Plants, fruits, seeds, snakes, fish, frogs

That's
Fact-tastic!

Black rhinos grow the **LONGEST HORNS** of any rhino species. Their front horn can reach up to five feet (1.5 m)—**LONGER THAN** an **EIGHT-YEAR-OLD KID IS TALL!** Rhinos use their horns for defending their territory, protecting their calves, and foraging for food.

RHINOCEROS

A **male rhinoceros the size of an SUV sniffs at a muddy** hollow in the ground. Then he gently lowers himself to the ground and rolls his enormous bulk in the mud. He's wallowing, a rhino's favorite daytime activity. This behavior helps these huge animals cool off and protects their skin from the sun and biting bugs, too.

There are five species of rhinoceros. Black and white rhinos live in Africa. Sumatran, Javan, and Indian (or greater one-horned) rhinos live in Asia. They are some of the most massive animals in the world. The largest, the white rhino, can weigh 5,000 pounds (2,300 kg). Rhinos get their name from their horns: The word "rhinoceros" means "nose-horn" in Greek. White rhinos, black rhinos, and Sumatran rhinos have two horns. Greater one-horned rhinos and Javan rhinos have one.

Unfortunately, the rhinos' most famous feature has put them in danger. Though rhino horns are made of keratin, like human fingernails, some people believe they have special healing powers. Rhinos are hunted for their horns, and three species—the black, Javan, and Sumatran—are critically endangered today. But all five species are in trouble: While there were about 500,000 rhinos in the wild at the beginning of the 20th century, there are only around 27,000 today.

Rhinos have a reputation as bad-tempered animals. But the true culprit is the animals' poor vision: Rhinos are very nearsighted, and they often charge at boulders or trees, mistaking them for attackers. Because they can't see oncoming danger very well, rhinos have learned to listen to the alarm calls of other animals, such as that of the oxpecker bird. In fact, the oxpecker's Swahili name, *Askari wa kifaru*, translates to "rhino's guard."

FACTS

SCIENTIFIC NAME Rhinocerotidae (family)

GROUP NAME Crash

SIZE Up to 13 feet (4 m)

WEIGHT Up to 5,000 pounds (2,300 kg)

EATS Grasses, leaves, shrubs

Rhinos' **SKIN** may resemble a **SUIT OF ARMOR**, but it's actually quite sensitive. Rhinos can **GET SUNBURNED!**

GIRAFFE

FACTS

SCIENTIFIC NAME *Giraffa camelopardalis*

GROUP NAME Herd

SIZE Up to 19 feet (5.8 m) tall

WEIGHT Up to 2,800 pounds (1,270 kg)

EATS Leaves, buds

ROTHSCHILD'S GIRAFFE

To fuel their big bodies on a **DIET OF LEAVES**, giraffes must spend **16 TO 20 HOURS** a day **EATING**.

Everything about giraffes is long. Their six-foot (1.8-m) legs are longer than the average human is tall. Their necks could allow the animals to peer through a second-story window. Even their tongues are long: 21 inches (53 cm), longer than two pencils placed end to end!

Giraffes' unique height allows them to easily graze on leaves and buds in treetops, where few other animals can reach. Acacia trees are one of a giraffe's favorite foods—but they are covered in thorns! Giraffes use their long tongues to pull the leaves off around the sharp bits, and they have tough mouths that can stand up to the occasional wayward thorn. But the acacias have a defense: They release bitter-tasting chemicals that discourage eating. The trees are also home to colonies of stinging ants. The ants live in the tree's hollow thorns and drink its nectar. In return, when a giraffe begins munching, they swarm into its eyes, ears, and nose.

Giraffes are so big that they have few animals to fear: Lions and crocodiles are their only natural predators. If threatened, their first instinct is to run. Giraffes have an unusual way of moving, with both front and back legs on one side swinging together at once. This strange gait allows them to reach speeds around 35 miles an hour (56 km/h) for short distances. If cornered, they'll defend themselves with a deadly, karate-style kick.

A giraffe's height, along with its excellent vision, makes it easy for this animal to spot approaching predators. Some scientists believe that other, shorter animals, such as zebras and antelope, gather near where giraffes are grazing to use the taller animals as a warning system. If a giraffe takes off running, the other grazers do, too!

ROTHSCHILD'S GIRAFFES

That's
Fact-tastic!

Giraffes have a reputation for being nearly **SILENT,** but **THEY'RE NOT.** Scientists spent eight years **RECORDING** giraffes in zoos and **DISCOVERED** that the animals do indeed **MAKE NOISE.** They spend their **NIGHTS HUMMING SONGS** at such a **LOW FREQUENCY** that humans can barely hear them.

NEED FOR
SPEED

CHEETAH

PRONGHORN ANTELOPE

Everyone knows the world's fastest land animal is the cheetah … right? It's true, but it's not the whole story. Cheetahs are incredibly fast, able to reach speeds of more than 60 miles an hour (97 km/h), faster than any other land animal on the planet. But they are only able to maintain this blistering pace for about 2,000 feet (600 m). Put a cheetah head-to-head in a distance race against the fastest hoofed animal, and the big cat will be left in the dust.

Pronghorn antelope, which live on the plains of North America, can sprint at speeds of more than 53 miles an hour (85 km/h), nearly as fast as a cheetah. And when running at the slightly slower pace of 45 miles an hour (72 km/h), pronghorn can hoof it for miles! While a cheetah may be a champion sprinter, the pronghorn is both a sprinter and a marathoner.

Hoofed animals are built for speed. From horses to wildebeest, many evade predators on open grassland by outrunning them. Their long legs allow them to cover lots of ground with every stride. They also run on their toes. (A hoof is a toe that has evolved over time to become enlarged and hardened.) That allows them to use fewer muscles when moving, helping them save energy so they can cover more distance than other animals.

Hoofed animals have other adaptations that increase their speed, too. Researchers have found that, pound for pound, pronghorn antelope consume far more oxygen when breathing than other animals. Specially adapted muscles help them burn that oxygen efficiently, turning it into energy that gives the antelope a speed boost.

This ability for speed starts when hoofed animals are just babies. Pronghorn females hide their little fawns in tall grass when they are born to protect them from predators. But within a few days, a fawn can outrun a human. Within weeks, they can outrun the coyotes, bobcats, and golden eagles that hunt them.

Why are **PRONGHORN ANTELOPE SO MUCH FASTER** than the hunters they need to outpace? **SCIENTISTS THINK** the answer is that the **PRONGHORN EVOLVED TO BEAT OUT AN EXTINCT PREDATOR**—possibly a long-legged big cat that could have been as fast as a modern cheetah.

QUARTER HORSE

WORLD'S FASTEST MAMMALS

These creatures give the rest of the animal kingdom a run for their money.

CHEETAH

In 2012, a cheetah from the Cincinnati Zoo ran a 100-meter dash in 5.95 seconds. Olympian Usain Bolt ran the same race in 9.58 seconds.

QUARTER HORSE

Named for its great speed over the short distance of a quarter mile, the quarter horse is a breed that has been clocked at 55 miles an hour (89 km/h).

PRONGHORN ANTELOPE

A pronghorn could cover the length of a football field in 3.5 seconds—in just 10 strides!

BLUE WILDEBEEST

This creature may look a bit like a buffalo, but it's actually a type of antelope capable of running at 50 miles an hour (80 km/h).

BLUE WILDEBEEST

That's **Fact-tastic!**

Warthogs have an **ABILITY** to **ADAPT** to **NEW THREATS** that helps these animals thrive. For example, most warthogs **FORAGE** during the **EARLY MORNINGS** and **EVENINGS**. But if they **LIVE** in a **DANGEROUS AREA**, they'll switch to **FORAGING AT NIGHT** when the darkness provides cover.

WARTHOG

With their curling tusks, patchy tufts of hair, and wartlike growths that cover their faces, warthogs aren't exactly known for their beauty. But they are tough, adaptable animals that thrive in their African home, where many other animals are threatened.

Despite their sharp tusks and teeth, warthogs are not ferocious creatures. They eat plants and also use their snouts to dig for roots and bulbs. If they have to, they can survive for months without water. But when they find water—or even a mud hole—they like to submerge themselves. This helps them cool down and also rid themselves of pesky biting insects. When it comes time to find shelter in the savanna, woodlands, and grasslands of much of sub-Saharan Africa where they live, warthogs don't bother to waste time and energy digging their own dens. Instead, they take over empty aardvark dens. Warthogs use these dens to rest, to give birth to their young, and as a place to hide. The animals usually enter their dens rear end first, putting their tusks at the entrance to scare off any nearby predators.

All kinds of animals, including lions, leopards, hyenas, and eagles, consider a warthog a tasty snack. When in danger, warthogs usually try to run. They are agile and swift, reaching speeds of up to 34 miles an hour (55 km/h). Warthogs run with their tails sticking straight up, like a tiny flag! If they need to, they can fight, using their sharp lower canine teeth as weapons and squealing as loudly as they can.

Warthogs are noisy animals. The females, called sows, live in groups of up to 40 with their young, and they use all kinds of vocalizations to communicate, from snorts and squeals to grunts and growls. Boars—male warthogs—live solitary lives, coming close to other warthogs only when it's time to mate. Then they battle to see who is biggest and strongest, ramming each other with their heads and tusks. Their fleshy "warts" protect the boars during battle—they're not just for looks after all!

FACTS

SCIENTIFIC NAME *Phacochoerus africanus*

GROUP NAME Sounder

SIZE About 30 inches (76 cm) at the shoulder

WEIGHT Up to 250 pounds (113 kg)

EATS Plants, grasses, roots, bulbs

As soon as a warthog **WAKES UP**, it **RUSHES OUT** of its **DEN** at **TOP SPEED** in case a **PREDATOR** is **WAITING**.

79

TAPIR

FACTS

SCIENTIFIC NAME Tapiridae (family)

GROUP NAME Candle

SIZE Up to 3.5 feet (1.1 m) at the shoulder

WEIGHT Up to 800 pounds (363 kg)

EATS Leaves, twigs, fruit, grasses

Is it a pig with an anteater's snout? No, it's a tapir! These animals are actually related to horses and rhinoceroses. Tapirs belong to an ancient lineage that has been around for about 20 million years and changed very little over that time. They are considered the most primitive large mammals in the world.

The tapir's long snout is actually a trunk, like a smaller version of an elephant's. It's prehensile, or gripping, and the tapir uses it like a hand: to grab branches and strip the leaves off or to pick fruit and put it directly in the tapir's mouth. The trunk is not just an extra limb; it's also a sensitive smelling organ that helps tapirs find food in the dark of night, when they like to feed. Tapirs can even use their trunk like a snorkel to help them breathe when underwater!

There are four species of tapir. Three of them live in Central and South America, and the fourth, the Malayan tapir, lives in Asia. Tapirs make their home in wetlands, forests, rainforests, and savannas. They stay near water, which they use for cooling off, getting rid of pests, and taking a nighttime dip. Scientists think that, like hippos (p. 88), tapirs don't really swim. Instead, they sink to the bottom of rivers and lakes, then walk across.

Tapirs play an important role in maintaining the health of their homes. They eat seeds and then travel through the forest. When they poop, they leave the seeds behind, in areas far from the parent plant. Their poop even acts like fertilizer, giving the seeds nutrients to help them grow. One study of tapirs in Peru found that their dung contained 122 different species of seed. That's some powerful poo!

The **TAPIR'S NOSE** is so **LONG** and **FLEXIBLE** that the animal can use it to **INVESTIGATE** a **CIRCLE** of ground **ONE FOOT** (30 cm) across.

BAIRD'S TAPIR

BRAZILIAN TAPIR CALF

That's Fact-tastic!

BABY TAPIRS look a little like **BROWN WATERMELONS** with spotted legs. This coloration helps them **HIDE** in the **SPOTTY, OR DAPPLED, LIGHT** in the forest. After about **SIX MONTHS,** young tapirs **LOSE THESE MARKINGS** and resemble small adults.

BUFFALO
VS. BISON

AFRICAN BUFFALO

Home, home on the range. **Enormous** Horned animals roam the plains of North America. Sometimes these big, furry beasts are called buffalo, and sometimes they're called bison. Which is correct?

Bison and buffalo are two different kinds of animal. There are two main species of buffalo: African buffalo (*Syncerus caffer*), which live in Africa, and water buffalo (*Bubalus arnee*), which live in Asia. No buffalo has ever walked the range in North America.

The hoofed-and-horned animals there are American bison (*Bison bison*).

Why the confusion? Historians think early European settlers to America are the reason. When they saw herds of bison, they may have called them "buffalo" due to their similar

WATER BUFFALO

Bison have a large hump of muscles on their shoulders. Combined with their massive heads, this makes their hind ends look smaller than their front ends.

A bison's horns usually grow to about two feet (0.6 m) long.

BISON

Their thick coat keeps bison warm in the cold winters on the Great Plains. They shed it for the warm season.

Bison have a long, shaggy beard.

appearance to the animals in Asia and Africa. Or perhaps the name grew from the French word for "beef," *boeuf*. No matter the reason for the mistake, it has stuck around to today.

Bison are the largest land animals in North America, clocking in at 1,000 to 2,200 pounds (500–1,000 kg) and standing up to six feet (1.8 m) tall. They feed on grasses, herbs, shrubs, and twigs. In the winter, they use their huge heads as snowplows to uncover plants to eat. Despite their enormous size, bison are extremely fast, able to reach speeds of 40 miles an hour (64 km/h). Their speed combined with their sharp horns—which are used for battling other bison—add up to one formidable animal.

North America's Indigenous people hunted bison for food and skins for generations. But they never killed enough of the animals to damage their population. At one time, there were as many as 60 million bison roaming the Great Plains. But when European settlers arrived with horses and guns, they began hunting bison for food, for their skins, and for sport. By the 1900s, there were fewer than 1,000 of the animals left.

Conservationists—many working with Native American tribes—stepped in to change that, and bison are now making a comeback. Though they inhabit just about one percent of their former range, there are now bison herds in parts of Canada and the American West. There are about 13,000 American bison in the wild today.

BISON

A **BISON'S COAT** is so **THICK** that **SNOW** can **COLLECT** on its **BACK WITHOUT MELTING.**

A buffalo's horns can be more than three feet (1 m) across. They form an upward curving shape.

Buffalo have a more symmetrical appearance.

BUFFALO

Their thinner coat does not shed.

Buffalo have no beard.

MUSK OX

FACTS

SCIENTIFIC NAME *Ovibos moschatus*

GROUP NAME Herd

SIZE Up to 5 feet (1.5 m) at the shoulder

WEIGHT Up to 800 pounds (363 kg)

EATS Roots, mosses, lichens, grasses, flowers

I t's winter on the Arctic tundra. With its breath steaming from its nostrils, the musk ox scrapes at the snow with a hoof, looking for moss and lichens—among the only edible plants that can survive here this time of year. While the environment is frigid, it's exactly where the musk ox is adapted to thrive.

Musk oxen are perfectly suited for life in the Arctic. Their shaggy hair is so long it nearly reaches the ground. It's made of two layers: Outer hairs called guard hairs protect a shorter undercoat that provides extra insulation during the winter. When winter ends, the undercoat sheds to keep the ox from overheating. During the summer, musk oxen graze on flowers and grasses, storing large amounts of fat that they rely on to survive the long winters. Musk oxen conserve energy in the cold season by slowing their breathing, heart rate, and digestion. They also spend as much time as possible staying very still.

Musk oxen face ferocious predators: bears and wolves. To protect themselves against attacks, the oxen use teamwork. They form a circle with their young in the middle and their sharp horns facing outward. When threatened, musk oxen aren't afraid to charge. Their massive bodies, weighing up to 800 pounds (363 kg), make this an intimidating sight!

Musk oxen have existed for thousands of years. During the Pleistocene epoch, which lasted from about 2.6 million to about 12,000 years ago, they roamed all across the Arctic region. But humans hunted them, and by the 1920s, they had disappeared from Arctic Alaska. Conservationists stepped in, and today musk oxen are on the rise, with populations in Alaska once more.

During mating season, **MALE MUSK OXEN CHARGE** each other at **SPEEDS** of up to **25 MILES AN HOUR (40 km/h)** and **SMASH** their **HORNS** together. They repeat this until one **BULL BACKS DOWN.**

That's
Fact-tastic!

Though these animals are called musk **"OXEN,"** they are **NOT CLOSELY RELATED** to oxen at all. (Oxen are cattle that have been trained to pull heavy loads.) Instead, **MUSK OXEN** are much more closely **RELATED** to **GOATS** and sheep.

HOOFING IT

Every year, millions upon millions of hooves drum the earth in the African Serengeti. It's the great wildebeest migration, the largest gathering of animals on the planet. More than 1.5 million wildebeest, accompanied by about 500,000 gazelles and 200,000 zebras, travel about 600 miles (1,000 km) across Africa from the Serengeti in Tanzania to the Masai Mara in Kenya. They are following the rains, moving toward fresh grazing land to keep themselves alive.

It's a dangerous journey. When the animals reach the Mara River, hundreds of crocodiles are waiting to make a meal out of them. When they reach the Masai Mara, they must travel through one of the largest concentrations of lions in the world. All along the way, predators like cheetahs, hyenas, and leopards are stalking the herd, watching for any migrator to show signs of weakness. These hoofed voyagers battle not just predators but also thirst, starvation, fatigue, and disease. Every year, about 250,000 animals perish along the way. Yet in the fall, the animals will return to the Serengeti once more, ready to begin again the following year.

All kinds of animals, from whales to birds to ladybugs, are known for their epic

Southern right WHALE MIGRATIONS cover more than 3,100 MILES (5,000 km) every YEAR.

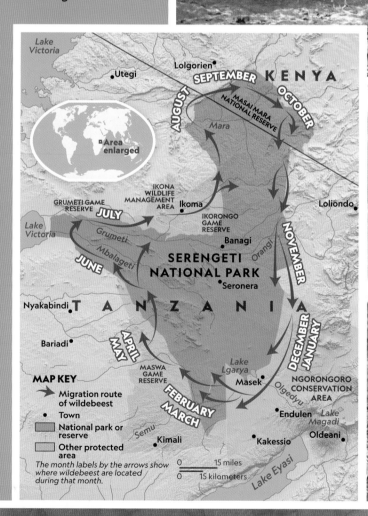

MAP KEY

→ Migration route of wildebeest
• Town
National park or reserve
Other protected area

The month labels by the arrows show where wildebeest are located during that month.

Lake Victoria
Utegi
Lolgorien
KENYA
SEPTEMBER
AUGUST
OCTOBER
MASAI MARA NATIONAL RESERVE
Mara
Area enlarged
IKONA WILDLIFE MANAGEMENT AREA
GRUMETI GAME RESERVE
JULY
Ikoma
IKORONGO GAME RESERVE
Loliondo
Lake Victoria
Grumeti
Banagi
NOVEMBER
Mbalageti
Orangi
JUNE
SERENGETI NATIONAL PARK
Seronera
Nyakabindi
T A N Z A N I A
Bariadi
APRIL MAY
Lake Lgarya
DECEMBER JANUARY
MASWA GAME RESERVE
Masek
NGORONGORO CONSERVATION AREA
Olgedyu
Lake Magadi
FEBRUARY MARCH
Endulen
Semu
Kimali
Kakessio
Oldeani
Lake Eyasi

0   15 miles
0   15 kilometers

MAKING SENSE OF MIGRATORS

All over the world, scientists marvel at animal migrations. What makes animals begin their yearly journeys? And how do they find their way? To answer these questions and others, scientists fit migrators with tracking collars. Using antennas or satellites, they can monitor the animals as they travel to uncover the secrets of their journeys.

So far, scientists have learned that different animals use different signals to decide when to migrate. Some rely on the amount of daylight. When days begin to get shorter, they know it's time to head to a new location for the winter. Other animals react to temperature, and still others use internal signals that aren't fully understood. To navigate, they may use the sun, the moon, and the stars, or even Earth's magnetic field.

WILDEBEEST

CARIBOU

migrations that can take them thousands of miles across the planet. But on land, it's the hoofed animals that rule migration. Mule deer travel from the Red Desert of Wyoming to Island Park, Idaho, U.S.A., crossing two highways and traveling 480 miles (770 km) every year. Two herds of caribou have been tracked making their way 840 miles (1,350 km) across northern North America—the equivalent of walking from Washington, D.C., to Tallahassee, Florida!

Much about migration is a mystery. Migrations seem to begin when a few animals decide, seemingly out of nowhere, to start moving. When migrating animals are on the move, nothing can distract them from their final goal—they travel in a straight line even when tasty food tempts them to go off course. It's no wonder the great wildebeest migration is considered one of the great wonders of the natural world.

That's
Fact-tastic!

Hippos sweat, but their sweat isn't like yours. Instead, they **SECRETE** an **OILY RED SUBSTANCE** that acts like **SUNBLOCK** and skin **MOISTURIZER** in one. Because of this unusual adaptation, some people **MISTAKENLY BELIEVE** that **HIPPOS SWEAT BLOOD.**

HIPPO-POTAMUS

The hippo rests in the cool water, its nose, ears, and eyes peeking above the surface. Hippos love water and spend most of their day submerged—that's why their name originates with the Greek words for river (*potamus*) and horse (*hippos*).

Despite their water-loving lifestyle, hippos can't swim—or even float. Instead, they move around by "bouncing" off the bottom of lakes and rivers on their toes in a slow-motion gallop. They can also dive down beneath the surface, their nose and ears closing to keep the water out. Hippos can hold their breath for about five minutes during a dive. Hippos can even sleep underwater! A special reflex allows them to rise to the surface, take a breath, and then sink back down without waking up. Now that's a deep sleep!

Hippos risk dehydration when they stay out of the water for too long. So they spend up to 16 hours a day submerged, a behavioral adaptation that keeps their big bodies cool under the hot sun of their African home. At dusk, when the air cools, hippos finally leave the water. It's time to eat! They can travel six miles (10 km) in a night, grazing on about 80 pounds (36 kg) of grass.

Hippos' roly-poly bodies may make them appear cute. But these are not animals to mess with. They weigh up to 8,000 pounds (3,6300 kg) and can be very aggressive when threatened. Their teeth never stop growing throughout their lives and can reach 20 inches (51 cm) in length. To tell enemies to back off, hippos open their mouths and yawn, shake their heads, or roar. If they have to, they will charge at up to 30 miles an hour (48 km/h)—an impressive speed for such an enormous animal!

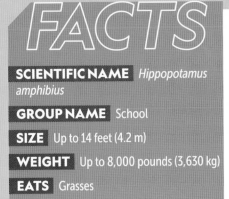

FACTS

SCIENTIFIC NAME *Hippopotamus amphibius*

GROUP NAME School

SIZE Up to 14 feet (4.2 m)

WEIGHT Up to 8,000 pounds (3,630 kg)

EATS Grasses

A hippo's **WIDE MOUTH** acts like a **LAWN MOWER** to chomp down **GRASS.**

PRZEWALSKI'S HORSE

FACTS

SCIENTIFIC NAME *Equus ferus przewalskii*

GROUP NAME Herd

SIZE Up to 4.7 feet (1.4 m) at the shoulder

WEIGHT Up to 750 pounds (340 kg)

EATS Grasses, leaves

Unlike other horses, **PRZEWALSKI'S HORSES SHED** their **MANE** and **TAIL** each year.

It's often called the last truly wild horse on planet Earth. The Przewalski's (shuh-VAL-skee's) horse is smaller than most domesticated horses, with a short, muscular body, striped legs, and a dark mane that stands straight up.

This lineage of horse is very ancient; cave paintings in Spain, Italy, and France that are more than 20,000 years old depict horses with the features of a Przewalski's horse. And herds of them once roamed throughout Europe and Asia, too. In the thousands of years these horses have lived, some experts think no human has ever managed to domesticate the Przewalski's horse or its ancestors. Other scientists disagree. They say Przewalski's horses are actually feral, or descended from domesticated ancestors that later returned to the wild.

The Przewalski's horse was not widely known until the late 19th century, when a Russian explorer spotted one and shared his observation with scientists. By the 1960s, it was completely driven to extinction in its natural habitat. But since then, conservationists have carefully bred Przewalski's horses in captivity and reintroduced them to small parts of Mongolia, China, Russia, and Kazakhstan. It's a cold and harsh place to make a home, but Przewalski's horses are perfectly adapted: They grow thick coats and even long beards for the winter.

Przewalski's horses have home ranges that can extend to 12 square miles (32 sq km), and they spend their days hoofing their way from one grazing spot to the next. They live in groups of up to 10 mares and their foals, led by one dominant stallion. The horses in a herd are very closely bonded: They eat at the same time, rest at the same time, and even give each other back scratches by nibbling their herd mates with their teeth.

That's Fact-tastic!

PRZEWALSKI'S **HORSES** are often called the **ONLY WILD HORSES** to exist in modern times. The **MUSTANGS** that roam North America and the **WILD HORSES** of Australia are actually **DESCENDANTS** of **DOMESTIC HORSES** that **ESCAPED RANCHES** and returned to the **WILD.**

THE **CAMEL FAMILY**

DROMEDARY CAMELS

A line of camels winds across the Sahara, sand stretching around the plodding animals in every direction. Modern camels and their relatives live only in Africa and Asia. But many people don't know that camels actually originated in North America.

There are two types of camels. Bactrian camels, which have two humps, live in the cold Gobi desert of Mongolia and China. Dromedary camels, which have one hump, live in the deserts of Africa and the Middle East. Camels belong to a family called Camelidae, along with llamas, alpacas, vicuñas, and guanacos. Their ancestor first appeared in North America about 45 million years ago. One early camel genus was *Camelops*, which resembled modern camels but was a bit taller at seven feet (2.1 m) at the shoulder. Like today's camels, *Camelops* did not have hooves. Instead, it had two hardened toes with thick nails and soles. One set of fossilized *Camelops* tracks

at White Sands National Park in New Mexico, U.S.A., stretches for more than two miles (3.2 km).

Camelops lived only in North America. But other ancient camels traveled into South America. These were the relatives of the llamas, alpacas, vicuñas, and guanacos that live there now. One extinct South American species, *Macrauchenia*, looked like a llama but had a long snout like an anteater! Still other camel species made their way into Asia, probably over a land bridge that connected North America and Asia during the last ice age.

Early humans also used this land bridge, called the Bering Land Bridge, to make their way across the world—but they went in the opposite direction, from Asia to North America. Our ancestors would have lived alongside ancient camels like *Camelops,* which went extinct only about 12,000 years ago.

DROMEDARY CAMELS

BACTRIAN CAMEL

Though camels can go weeks without drinking water, they don't store water in their humps. **CAMEL HUMPS HOLD FAT.** When needed, **CAMELS** can **BREAK DOWN** this **FAT INTO WATER** and energy, giving them the ability to travel up to 100 miles (160 km) without drinking.

CAMEL COUSINS

These camel relatives all make their home in the Andes mountains of South America.

ALPACAS

Smaller than llamas, at around three feet (1 m) at the shoulders, alpacas are known for their soft wool, which is used to make clothing and blankets.

LLAMAS

Llamas are the largest of the South American Camelidae, at four feet (1.3 m) at the shoulder. They were domesticated about 5,000 years ago to be pack animals—animals that carry supplies for humans. Llamas are still the only way to get around in some parts of the steep, remote Andes!

GUANACOS

Guanacos are just a bit smaller than llamas, and they look similar to them. But whereas llamas can have coats in a range of colors, all guanacos are brown with white underparts.

VICUÑAS

Considered a symbol of Peru, this wild creature is small in size at just around 2.5 feet (0.8 m). Its wool, used to weave sweaters, blankets, and other fabrics, is incredibly soft.

That's
Fact-tastic!

An elephant's **HUGE EARS** help **COOL** the animal down. They contain many blood vessels that carry blood close to the skin's surface. When an elephant **FLAPS ITS EARS,** this **COOLS THE BLOOD,** which flows to the rest of its body. **COOL TRICK!**

SAVANNA ELEPHANT

A herd of elephants travels across the savanna. **As they** walk, their footsteps shake the ground. The mighty African savanna elephant is the largest land mammal on Earth, with legs the size of tree trunks, and ears taller than the average human. Even an elephant's eyelashes are supersize, at five inches (13 cm) long—about as long as a can of soda is tall!

An elephant's trunk has many uses. Besides being a smelling organ, it is an extra limb so strong it can push down a tree. It also has two "fingers" at the tip that can perform delicate maneuvers like plucking a single blade of grass. An elephant's trunk can also act as a straw, able to suck up water—as much as two gallons (7.6 L) at a time—and then blow the water down the elephant's mouth. A trunk can be a hose, used to spray water or dust over an elephant's body to protect its skin. It can be a snorkel that allows an elephant to breathe when underwater. Elephants even wrap their trunks together to "hug."

Elephant herds are matriarchal, meaning that they are led by a female—usually the biggest and oldest. She remembers important information—like where to find water in the dry season—and uses her knowledge to help her herd survive. The herd is made up of other female elephants, called cows, and their young. Adult male elephants, called bulls, usually roam on their own.

Elephants are essential parts of their ecosystem. They shape the land around them, using their trunks to dig up dry riverbeds to create watering holes that are used by many animals. They also clear small trees, which keeps the savanna open for grazers such as zebras and antelope. That's why elephants are sometimes called "ecosystem engineers"!

FACTS

SCIENTIFIC NAME *Loxodonta africana*

GROUP NAME Herd

SIZE Up to 13 feet (4 m) at the shoulder

WEIGHT Up to 7 tons (6.5 t)

EATS Roots, grasses, fruit, bark

BABY ELEPHANTS SUCK THEIR TRUNKS just like HUMAN BABIES SUCK their THUMBS.

95

ELK

FACTS

SCIENTIFIC NAME *Cervus canadensis*

GROUP NAME Gang

SIZE Up to 5 feet (1.5 m) at the shoulder

WEIGHT Up to 1,100 pounds (500 kg)

EATS Grasses, other plants

An adult male elk delicately picks his way through the forest, pausing with ears forward to listen for any hints of danger. Elk are graceful animals that can move nearly soundlessly. This makes it easy to overlook that they are also enormous: Counting its antlers, a male elk can be nine feet (2.7 m) tall!

Elk antlers—which are made of bone and grown only by the males, or bulls—are a marvel of biology. Unlike an elephant's tusks, which grow throughout its life, elk antlers fall off in the springtime, then begin to grow back in preparation for the breeding season in late summer. To reach full size in just a few months, the antlers must grow incredibly fast: up to one inch (2.5 cm) a day! Scientists have found that the same genes that cause this rapid growth can also cause cancer in humans. They are studying this elk ability for clues about how to fight cancer.

When the breeding season begins, bull elk prepare by rubbing the soft "velvet" coating off their antlers. They charge at competing bulls and crash their antlers together in a battle for access to the females. The older animals—which usually have the biggest antlers—typically win. From dawn to dusk during this time, the air is full of the sound of elk bugling. Researchers were confused about how elk produce this strange sound—which can sound like a high-pitched scream— until they realized the elk were both roaring and whistling at the same time.

Elk live all over the world, with large populations mostly in North America. They are sometimes called *wapiti,* a word in the language of some Indigenous people that refers to their white rumps. In the culture of many Native American groups, elk are connected with love and music.

An elk's **ANTLERS** can weigh **40 POUNDS** (18 kg)— about the **WEIGHT** of a **FIVE-YEAR-OLD KID.**

That's Fact-tastic!

An elk's **BUGLE** is a **SOUND** that can **TRAVEL** for **MILES.** But **RESEARCHERS** have found that the animals **COMMUNICATE** with another sound, too: Their **ANKLEBONES** make a **CRACKING SOUND** when they walk that other **ELK RECOGNIZE.**

AMAZING ANTELOPE

Antelope are not one kind of animal. Instead, they are a whole group of grazing, fleet-footed ungulates. Africa is home to some 70 species of antelope, and they range all the way from its jungles to its vast desert, the Sahara.

THOMSON'S GAZELLE

Unusual for herd animals, Thomson's gazelles are constantly leaving their group and joining a new one. During the rainy season, thousands of Thomson's gazelles can be spotted gathering on the grasslands of East Africa. There in the open, they are vulnerable to predators like cheetahs, but this gazelle can usually race away at a speedy 40 miles an hour (64 km/h).

SPRINGBOK

BOING! A springbok bounces across the landscape, jumping with stiff legs, an arched back, and all four feet off the ground. This strange behavior is called pronking, and no one is sure why some antelope do it. Perhaps it's a way to confuse predators, perhaps it helps attract other springbok—or perhaps it's just for fun!

ADDAX

With its snow-white coat and its long, spiraling horns, the addax is one of the most unusual antelope species. Addax live in arid regions of northern Africa, where their long, flat hooves act a bit like snowshoes, helping them walk across sand without sinking. The addax once ranged from the Atlantic Ocean to the Nile River, but is now critically endangered, with fewer than about 100 animals left. Conservationists are working to breed them in captivity and bring them back to the wild.

GERENUK

Its name means "giraffe-necked" in Somali. And besides its long neck, the gerenuk also has a slender body and extremely long, thin legs. These lengthy limbs help the gerenuk reach the middle leaves of trees, an area too high up for other antelope and too low for giraffes. To give themselves an extra height boost, gerenuks sometimes feed while standing on their two hind legs.

ROYAL ANTELOPE

At just 10 inches (25 cm) tall and 5.5 to seven pounds (2.5—3 kg), this is the world's smallest antelope—no bigger than a rabbit. The royal antelope lives in dense vegetation at the forest floor in West Africa. Its nocturnal habits and shy nature mean that it's rarely spotted in the wild, and little is known about it. But stumble across one and it can leap away quickly, jumping up to eight feet (2.4 m) in a single bound!

SAIGA ANTELOPE

They're perhaps the world's weirdest antelope. The enormous, bulbous nose of the saiga antelope doesn't just make this ungulate look odd: Experts think it helps filter out dust in the summer and warm up cold air in the winter. Saiga antelope live on the steppes, or grasslands, of Central Asia, where they have survived largely unchanged for millions of years—these antelope once roamed alongside mammoths and saber-toothed cats!

CHINESE WATER DEER

FACTS

SCIENTIFIC NAME *Hydropotes inermis*

GROUP NAME None

SIZE Up to 3.3 feet (1 m)

WEIGHT Up to 31 pounds (14 kg)

EATS Grasses

A deer with fangs? This is no mammal monster: It's a Chinese water deer. Fanged deer, sometimes nicknamed "vampire deer," belong to several species, including water deer and musk deer. That's because the ancestor of all modern deer had both antlers and fangs. Most deer species grew larger antlers and lost their fangs, but the fanged deer did just the opposite: Some lost their antlers, and their upper canine teeth grew until they extended past the deer's jaw.

Despite their nickname, fanged deer don't lurk in the shadows, waiting to bite an unlucky victim and drain its blood. Instead, they use their two-inch (5-cm) fangs—actually called tusks—like other deer use their antlers: for fighting off rivals. And while these deer might look scary, they're small in size: Chinese water deer grow to only about 3.3 feet (1 m) tall at the shoulder and weigh up to 31 pounds (14 kg).

The Chinese water deer is native to China and Korea, where their coarse, thick coats and furry ears protect them from cold, snowy winters. There are also wild populations in the United Kingdom that got their start when captive water deer escaped from zoos and parks in the early 20th century. Except for during mating season, they are solitary animals. When threatened, they don't use their fangs for fighting, instead choosing to run away with bursts of speed.

Shy and secretive, water deer like to stay in the protection of lush vegetation near rivers. Here, their tusks don't seem strange at all; while antlers would get tangled, tusks allow the deer to slip through the foliage.

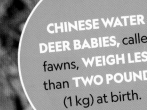

CHINESE WATER DEER BABIES, called fawns, WEIGH LESS than TWO POUNDS (1 kg) at birth.

That's
Fact-tastic!

The Chinese water deer's
TUSKS are HINGED. That
allows the deer to FOLD them
BACK slightly so they don't get
in the way WHILE the animal is
GRAZING. When the deer
wants to use the TUSKS AS
WEAPONS, it can PUSH
them FORWARD.

Zebras often **TEAM UP** with other **GRAZERS** such as **ANTELOPE** and **WILDEBEEST** as they **MIGRATE.** This helps keep them **SAFE FROM PREDATORS.** Still, **CROCODILES** and **BIG CATS** lie in wait, **ATTRACTED** to the **HUGE GATHERING** of **PREY** animals.

PLAINS ZEBRA

During their yearly migration in the Serengeti (p. 86), tens of thousands of plains zebras can gather together. Looking at this sea of stripes, it can be hard to tell where one zebra ends and the next begins! But each zebra's stripes are as unique as a human fingerprint, with no two animals having the exact same pattern.

Nearly all mammals on Earth, from bears to elephants, have solid-color coats. So why are zebras so flashy? Scientists aren't sure! But they do have several theories. The bold black-and-white patterns may disorient predators by making it difficult to single out an individual animal from the herd. The stripes may also confuse insects and keep them from biting the zebras. And an individual zebra's particular stripe pattern may help the other members of its herd recognize it.

There are three species of zebra: the plains zebra, which is the most common; Grevy's zebra; and the mountain zebra. All live in Africa. Zebras are members of the horse family, and like horses, they are fast runners, able to reach speeds of up to 35 miles an hour (56 km/h). Also like horses, zebras live in herds, spending all of their time grazing on grass together and even using their teeth to groom each other. Usually, plains zebras live in small herds of several females and their young, along with a male, called a stallion, who stays at the back of the group to protect the rest from predators.

Zebras have many predators on the African plains, including lions and hyenas. Baby zebras are especially vulnerable, and so they are born nearly ready to flee from danger. A baby zebra can walk just 20 minutes after it's born. It can run after just one hour!

FACTS

SCIENTIFIC NAME *Equus quagga*
GROUP NAME Herd
SIZE Up to 5 feet (1.5 m) at the shoulder
WEIGHT Up to 990 pounds (450 kg)
EATS Grasses

Experts think that a **ZEBRA'S NIGHT VISION** is about as **GOOD AS** an **OWL'S.**

HOOFED ANIMALS
IN YOUR BACKYARD

Not all ungulates are wild creatures. Many familiar farm animals are hoofed, milk-drinking mammals. In fact, many domesticated animals are ungulates! Here are some of Earth's most familiar hoofed animals.

COW

There are a huge number of cows on the planet: one for every five people! They were first domesticated from a wild species of cattle called the aurochs, a large, horned creature often featured in the cave paintings of early humans. Modern cows are still impressively enormous: The tallest cow on record, named Blossom, stood 6.2 feet (1.9 m) tall at the shoulders.

SHEEP

In recent years, archaeologists investigating an early human settlement in Turkey found evidence that people kept wild sheep penned in their village an astounding 11,000 years ago. This makes sheep one of the earliest domesticated animals on Earth. Today, sheep are raised mostly for their wool. The wool of domestic sheep never stops growing: A single sheep can produce enough wool each year to make 300 miles (483 km) of yarn.

PIG

People might say they "sweat like a pig" on a hot day, but that's impossible—pigs have very few sweat glands. To cool off, they roll in mud, which gives them a mistaken reputation as dirty animals. Pigs are perhaps the most intelligent and highly trainable of all domesticated animals. People have taught pigs how to bowl, surf, and even play video games.

GOAT

There are three types of goats: domestic goats, which are the kind found on a farm; mountain goats, which inhabit the American Northwest; and wild goats, a group of many species which includes the strange, spiral-horned markhor goats of Asia. Goats are surprisingly intelligent: They are able to solve puzzles to receive treats. They also have incredible agility and balance: In Morocco, they're even known to climb trees!

DEER

Deer are the only group of animals in the world to have antlers. Unlike horns, antlers fall off and regrow every year—that makes them among the fastest-growing living tissue in the world. There are more than 40 species of deer in the world, and they are found on all continents except Australia and Antarctica. They can range from large to exceedingly small: The biggest deer species is the moose (p. 106), which towers over most humans at 6.5 feet (2 m) at the shoulder. The smallest deer, the southern pudu, is only about 14 inches (36 cm) tall.

MOOSE

FACTS

SCIENTIFIC NAME *Alces alces*

GROUP NAME Herd

SIZE Up to 6.5 feet (2 m) at the shoulder

WEIGHT Up to 1,800 pounds (815 kg)

EATS Twigs, shrubs, moss

A n animal one and a half times as heavy as a grand piano moves through the forest. It's a moose, the largest of all the deer species. Moose are truly enormous, with bodies that can reach 6.5 feet (2 m) at the shoulder—not including their heads or their huge antlers, which can be wider across than a refrigerator is tall.

Moose are so tall that bending down to eat grass isn't easy for them. Instead, they mostly feed on leaves, bark, and twigs from trees and shrubs. Their big size comes with a big appetite: Moose can chow down about 70 pounds (32 kg) of plant material per day in the summer, when food is plentiful. In the winter, they devour anything edible, including shrubs and pinecones. They also use their hooves to scrape away snow to get at mosses and lichens growing underneath. When the winter ice melts, moose often take to lakes and rivers to snack on aquatic plants. Even though they are so huge, moose are good swimmers that can paddle for miles and even submerge themselves underwater! Besides their bulk, moose have adaptations that help them fight off predators. When threatened, they will lash out with their large, sharp hooves. One kick can be fatal to a predator such as a wolf or bear. Moose don't usually use their antlers to fend off attackers. Instead, a male moose will display this impressive headgear to other males to show his superior strength and size in conflicts over mates. If one moose doesn't back down, the two huge creatures will smash their antlers together in battle.

A **MOOSE** has a **FLAP** of **SKIN** called a **BELL** that **DANGLES** beneath its **THROAT.**

That's Fact-tastic!

Almost all species of **MALE DEER GROW ANTLERS.** Unlike horns, **ANTLERS** are **SHED** each winter and **REGROWN** each spring. Each time antlers **REGROW,** they are **BIGGER** than they were before. A **MOOSE'S ANTLERS,** called **PADDLES,** can reach **SIX FEET** (1.8 m) from end to end!

EXTINCT UNGULATES

Not so very long ago, strange creatures hoofed their way across the planet. From woolly mammoths and prehistoric rhinoceroses to some of the largest land mammals ever to exist, the ungulates of the past were incredible animals.

QUAGGA

This subspecies of the plains zebra went extinct in the late 19th century. But scientists are now trying to bring it back. Quaggas had stripes like a zebra, but only on the front half of their bodies. They roamed South Africa until they were hunted to extinction around 1880. Scientists in South Africa are selectively breeding zebras with quagga traits, in the hopes of someday re-creating the animal.

WOOLLY MAMMOTH

Most of these prehistoric relatives of modern Asian elephants went extinct about 10,000 years ago. But scientists know a lot about them, because many mammoths were preserved in the permafrost, or permanently frozen ground, of the Arctic. They looked very much like their modern relatives, aside from their thick coats of brown hairs, which could be up to three feet (1 m) long, and their long tusks, which were used for fighting and digging and could grow to 15 feet (5 m) long.

CHALICOTHERE

This was one odd ungulate. Chalicothere was a horselike creature that stood 8.5 feet (2.6 m) high and weighed about 800 pounds (360 kg). But it didn't walk like a horse—instead, it ambled on its huge front knuckles. Unlike other ungulates, it didn't have hooves but rather claws, which it may have used to hook branches so it could pull them down to seek out the most tender leaves to eat.

PARACERATHERIUM

Measuring more than 26 feet (8 m) long and weighing perhaps as much as five elephants, *Paraceratherium* was an enormous rhinoceros that roamed Europe and Asia some 30 million years ago. Much about it remains a mystery to scientists. But they do think that, like a giraffe, it probably used its height and long neck to forage for leaves in the treetops.

WOOLLY RHINOCEROS

In 2020, researchers investigating a mummified puppy discovered that it had had an unusual last meal—a piece of meat from a woolly rhinoceros. These animals, which went extinct at the end of the Ice Age around 12,000 years ago, lived across Europe, North Africa, and Asia. They had two horns on their snout and a coat of thick fur, which helped protect them from the cold. Early humans often depicted woolly rhinos in their cave paintings.

CHAPTER **FOUR**

MAMMALS WITH POCKETS

MARSUPIALS

ALL ABOUT MARSUPIALS

They hop across grasslands, cling to tree trunks, and even glide through the air. They're the marsupials, or pouched mammals.

Marsupials have short pregnancies—the Virginia opossum, for example, carries her young inside her body for only 13 days! Baby marsupials are tiny when they are born, some no bigger than a grain of rice. These small, helpless creatures squirm their way through their mother's fur to her pouch. There, they nurse and grow until they are big and strong enough to leave the pouch.

Though many living marsupials make their home in Australia, this group of animals didn't get its start down under. Instead, scientists think that marsupials first appeared during the age of the dinosaurs, about 125 million years ago, in North America. From there, they made their way to South America, where they flourished. Even today, South America is home to more than 100 species of marsupials, mostly in the opossum family. Up until about 35 million years ago, South America and Australia were both connected to Antarctica, forming one huge landmass. Ancient marsupials traveled across this mega-continent from what is now South America to what is now Australia, where all sorts of species still live today. From tiny insect-eaters to large herbivores, from those that glide through the air to those that live underground, marsupials are a diverse group of animals!

BRUSH-TAILED BETTONG

SCIENTIFIC NAME: *Bettongia penicillata*

SIZE: Up to 15 inches (38 cm) with a 14-inch (36-cm) tail

WEIGHT: About 2.5 to 3.5 pounds (1.1–1.6 kg)

EATS: Fungi, bulbs, tubers, seeds, insects

COMMON SPOTTED CUSCUS

SCIENTIFIC NAME: *Spilocuscus maculatus*

SIZE: Up to 23 inches (58 cm) with a 17-inch (43-cm) tail

WEIGHT: Up to 13 pounds (6 kg)

EATS: Leaves

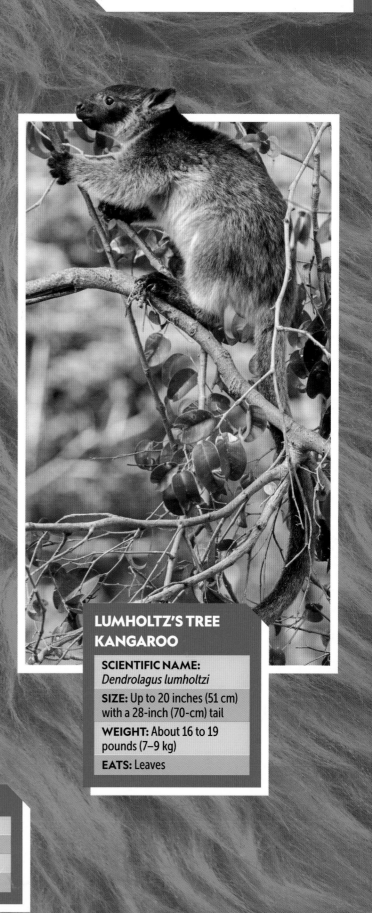

LUMHOLTZ'S TREE KANGAROO

SCIENTIFIC NAME: *Dendrolagus lumholtzi*

SIZE: Up to 20 inches (51 cm) with a 28-inch (70-cm) tail

WEIGHT: About 16 to 19 pounds (7–9 kg)

EATS: Leaves

BLACK AND RUFOUS ELEPHANT SHREW

SCIENTIFIC NAME: *Rhynchocyon petersi*

SIZE: Up to 12 inches (31 cm) with a 10-inch (25-cm) tail

WEIGHT: Up to 1.6 pounds (0.7 kg)

EATS: Insects

RED KANGAROO

SCIENTIFIC NAME *Macropus rufus*

GROUP NAME Mob

SIZE Up to 5.25 feet (1.6 m) with a 3.6-foot (1.1-m) tail

WEIGHT Up to 200 pounds (91 kg)

EATS Grasses

Kangaroos **CANNOT WALK FORWARD** or **BACKWARD**—they have to **HOP**.

Red kangaroos hop across the grasslands and deserts of Australia. They are the world's largest marsupials, standing about as tall as a human and weighing about 200 pounds (91 kg). Kangaroos are powerful animals, able to hop at speeds of more than 35 miles an hour (56 km/h) and cover 25 feet (7.6 m) in a single bound. That's like leaping over five queen-size mattresses laid side by side! Kangaroos are some of the planet's only bipedal marsupials—meaning that they move around on two legs instead of four.

Red kangaroos live together in groups called mobs, which usually have about 10 members. During droughts, thousands of kangaroos can come together at a water source. Kangaroos have several adaptations that help them survive Australia's extreme hot season. Unlike most mammals, they can sweat like humans do. They also have a network of blood vessels near the surface of the skin on their forearms. Licking their forearms helps cool this blood, keeping a kangaroo from overheating. Red kangaroos are also able to get both nutrition and water from the grasses and leaves that they eat.

It's common to see a kangaroo mother with the head or feet of her baby sticking out of her pouch. Young kangaroos are called joeys. When a joey is born, it's smaller than a cherry. The tiny baby crawls to its mother's pouch, where it stays for two months. Even after joeys have left the pouch to explore the world, they'll quickly dive back in at the slightest hint of danger.

Over the centuries, Australians have cleared native forests and woodlands, making it difficult for animals that depend on trees, such as gliders (p. 128), to survive. But since kangaroos need open grassland, land-clearing has helped kangaroo populations boom. Today, millions of these animals hop across Australian deserts and grasslands.

That's **Fact-tastic!**

MALE KANGAROOS will **"KICKBOX"** each other, leaning back on their **STRONG TAILS** so they can **PUMMEL** their opponents with their **FRONT LEGS** and **KICK** them with their **HIND LEGS**. It takes males **YEARS OF TRAINING** to learn how to **WIN** a **KICKBOXING** fight.

That's **Fact-tastic!**

The Tasmanian devil is called a **"GORGE EATER"** because when it finds a meal, it will **EAT UNTIL IT CAN'T EAT ANY MORE.** Devils can eat up to **40 PERCENT** of their **BODY WEIGHT** in one sitting. That's like a **SEVEN-YEAR-OLD EATING 40 BURGERS!**

TASMANIAN DEVIL

Tasmanian devils are known for their terrible tempers. And no wonder: Devils have a habit of opening their mouths wide when threatened. And when a group of them gathers to battle over food, they fill the air with chilling screeches and screams. But do they deserve their bad reputation?

Many of the Tasmanian devil's behaviors might seem scary. But to other devils, they're perfectly normal. The wide-open mouth pose expresses fear, not aggression. And the bone-chilling noises they make help them establish dominance and decide who gets to feed first. When devils face off, their ears turn red and they make a loud sneezing sound. It's all for show, however—most of the time, one devil will back down before a fight breaks out.

Tasmanian devils are found only on the island of Tasmania, off the southern coast of Australia. They rest during the day, snoozing under rocks or in caves or burrows. Then, at night, they emerge to hunt, traveling up to 10 miles (16 km) in search of food. As the world's largest carnivorous marsupials, Tasmanian devils eat birds, snakes, fish, and insects, as well as the carcasses of dead animals, called carrion. Devils will eat almost anything, no matter how decayed. And they'll consume every part of the animal, down to its hair and organs. Their oversize head, neck, and jaws are perfectly adapted for crunching bones.

These animals are tough from the day they're born. A mother devil will give birth to up to 50 young, called imps, at once. The itty-bitty devils are only about the size of a grain of rice, but they race to the mother's pouch and compete for one of her four teats. Only the four devils that win this competition will survive and grow up to prowl the Tasmanian night.

FACTS

SCIENTIFIC NAME *Sarcophilus harrisii*

GROUP NAME None

SIZE Up to 31 inches (79 cm)

WEIGHT Up to 26 pounds (11.8 kg)

EATS Birds, snakes, fish, insects, carrion

The Tasmanian devil's **OVERSIZE HEAD** houses **STRONG JAWS** that give it, pound for pound, one of the **MOST POWERFUL BITES** of any mammal.

MORE CARNIVOROUS MARSUPIALS

The always hungry Tasmanian devil isn't the only meat-eating marsupial on the planet. A whole family of these animals, called Dasyuridae, lives in Australia and New Guinea. They are all excellent hunters that rely on keen senses to overtake their prey.

EASTERN QUOLL

With their mouselike faces and bodies covered in white polka dots, eastern quolls may just be one of the continent's most adorable animals. So when they went extinct on mainland Australia some 50 years ago, people rallied together to do something. In March 2018, 20 quolls were transplanted from the island of Tasmania, where they still survived, back to Australia. Conservationists hope these omnivorous den-dwelling marsupials are home for good.

PLANIGALE

For much of every year, the sun bakes Australia's northern grasslands. Deep cracks develop in the soil—and they become the home for planigales. With their long, hairless tails, these creatures look a bit like mice, but they are the world's smallest marsupials. At night, planigales prowl the cracks in the earth to search for centipedes, spiders, small lizards, and other prey.

DUNNART

During the day, dunnarts curl up in little nests made of dried grass and leaves and snooze. But at night, these mouse-size marsupials emerge to become ferocious hunters. They catch and eat beetles, crickets, and even small mammals. They are hardy creatures able to survive without ever drinking water—they get all they need from their prey. They live all over Australia in a range of environments from forests to grasslands to deserts.

NUMBAT

The numbat is not like any other animal on Earth. Unlike nearly all other marsupials, it is active during the day, it has no pouch, and it eats only termites. The numbat has a long, pointed nose that it pokes into holes and under logs to sniff out its prey. Like an anteater, it has a long, sticky tongue that it uses to slurp up termites. A single numbat can eat around 20,000 termites in a day!

ANTECHINUS

Some of Earth's creatures use a once-in-a-lifetime strategy to pass on their genes: They mate only once, and then usually die. Salmon and mayflies do this, but it's rare among mammals. Only the antechinus and its relatives—small, insect-eating marsupials—reproduce this way. When the single litter of babies is born, there are a lot of them: Antechinuses have up to 14 little ones at a time, the biggest litter of any Australian marsupial.

That's
Fact-tastic!

All koalas have **WHITE FUR** on their **CHEST** and **RUMP**. But koalas in the **NORTHERN PART** of their territory have **SILVERY GRAY FUR,** and koalas that live in the **SOUTH,** closer to Antarctica, sometimes have **BROWNER, THICKER FUR.** Experts think that may be an **ADAPTATION** that helps them **SURVIVE** the colder **WINTERS.**

KOALA

Some people call these fuzzy creatures "koala bears." And like bears, koalas do have round ears, and they're covered with fur. But koalas aren't bears at all. Instead, they're marsupials. And even though they look soft, their fur is actually coarse, like a sheep's wool.

Koalas are native to southeastern and eastern Australia, where they live in eucalyptus forests. Koalas survive on a diet of eucalyptus leaves, which are stringy, tough, and filled with toxins. In fact, eucalyptus is so toxic that almost no other animals can eat it! Koalas have special adaptations that allow them to survive on this extreme diet. They can tell when the leaves have higher amounts of toxin and know to avoid them during that time. Koalas have special bacteria in their digestive systems that break down the toxic substances within the leaves so they aren't hurt by them. And they even have specialized teeth that help them grind up the leaves.

Koalas have unusual paws. On their hind paws, they have two toes that are fused together. They use these toes to comb their fur. And similar to a human, they have opposable thumbs that can close over their palms. But instead of just one thumb on each front paw, they have two! This helps them hold on to branches as they climb through the forest. It also helps them grip their food. Koalas can grab and eat more than a pound (0.5 kg) of eucalyptus leaves daily.

All that eating is tiring. When they're not chowing down, koalas are usually sleeping. Since eucalyptus isn't very nutritious, koalas have a lifestyle that helps them conserve energy: They sleep 20 hours a day.

FACTS

SCIENTIFIC NAME *Phascolarctos cinereus*

GROUP NAME None

SIZE Up to 33.5 inches (85 cm)

WEIGHT 20 pounds (9 kg)

EATS Eucalyptus leaves

Because they **EAT** so much **EUCALYPTUS**, **KOALAS** often **SMELL** like **COUGH DROPS.**

NIGHT LIFE

All around the world, marsupials wait for night to fall. When it does, they emerge from their hiding places. Some munch on plants, while others hunt for insects, reptiles, or mammals. The numbat (p. 119) and another species, the musky rat kangaroo, are the only marsupials that are diurnal (active during the day). All the rest are nocturnal (active at night) or crepuscular (active during twilight).

Nocturnal and crepuscular animals become more active when the sun goes down as a way to increase their odds of survival. A nighttime lifestyle allows animals such as kangaroos to stay out of the hot Australian sun. Other marsupials come out at night because darkness helps them hide from predators. And still others do it because darkness helps them sneak up on prey of their own.

Night-dwelling animals are specially adapted for living life in the dark: Many have large eyes with wide pupils to take in as much light as possible. But some nocturnal animals don't rely on their eyesight at all. Instead, they have large ears that help them navigate through the darkness using sounds. They also use sensitive whiskers to detect objects close by them. And many also have an excellent sense of smell: A special organ called the vomeronasal organ located in the roof of their mouth helps them sniff out food or mates.

All mammals were nocturnal until about 66 million years ago, when some slowly began adapting to daytime living. They began this switch just after the dinosaurs died out. Some experts believe this could mean that when dinosaurs walked the planet, mammals stayed safe by only coming out at night. Once the dinosaurs disappeared, mammals were free to roam in the daytime, too.

A majority of **MAMMALS** are **NOCTURNAL.**

BRUSH-TAIL POSSUM

WOMBAT

Many nocturnal animals have a **MEMBRANE** in their eyes that can make their **EYES APPEAR REFLECTIVE** when a bright light shines on them.

GREATER BILBY

THE NEW NIGHT OWLS

Most wild animals want to keep their distance from humans. But as people have moved into wild lands around the globe, many animals have been pushed to the limits of their ranges. They can't move any farther away, so instead they have shifted their schedules. In 2018, scientists released a study that showed mammals around the world that were once active during the day are becoming more and more nocturnal to avoid contact with people. Sun bears, for example, normally spend more than 80 percent of their active awake time during the day. But in areas where people are moving into the bears' range, sun bears are now spending nearly all of their waking time after dark.

WALLABY

FACTS

SCIENTIFIC NAME Macropodidae (family)

GROUP NAME Mob, court, troupe

SIZE Up to 3.4 feet (1 m) with a 29-inch (74-cm) tail

WEIGHT Up to 53 pounds (24 kg)

EATS Grasses, plants

Wallabies look like smaller versions of kangaroos. And although the two are closely related, wallabies aren't just a littler variety of their cousins.

While kangaroos inhabit open areas, wallabies have special adaptations that help them survive in forests. They have compact hind legs to help maneuver through the trees. They also have dappled coats, made up of reds, browns, and grays. This coloration helps disguise them as they lie in the shade when resting. And while kangaroos have sharp teeth for slicing grass, wallabies have flat teeth better for grinding up leaves.

Like kangaroos, wallabies move around by hopping. They use their large, powerful hind limbs to push off the ground. For humans, hopping is hard work. But these animals are specially adapted to their way of moving around. At the end of each bounce, energy collects in their legs, which they use to spring forward on the next bounce. Similar to how a pogo stick works, this allows wallabies to hop without using much energy. In fact, the faster they hop, the less energy they burn! They also use their long, thick tails to help them balance and turn as they go.

There are many species of wallaby that make their home in Australia and on its surrounding islands. Many are named for the habitats they live in, such as swamp wallabies and rock wallabies. There are also hare wallabies, named for their size and rabbitlike behavior, and even nailtail wallabies, named for a small spur-like growth at the tip of their tail. Wallabies can be nearly as big as a kangaroo or teeny tiny: The monjon, a type of rock wallaby, is 11.8 inches (30 cm) long and weighs 2.9 pounds (1.3 kg)—smaller than a Chihuahua.

MACROPODIDAE, the scientific name for the family of wallabies and kangaroos, MEANS "BIG FOOT"!

YELLOW-FOOTED ROCK WALLABY

That's **Fact-tastic!**

WALLABIES and **KANGAROOS** are known for hopping. But they can **ALSO CRAWL** on **ALL FOUR LEGS** and even **SWIM!** When they **HOP,** they **MOVE** their two back **LEGS TOGETHER.** But when they **SWIM,** their back **LEGS KICK INDEPENDENTLY.**

AGILE WALLABY

That's
Fact-tastic!

In 2014, **PALEONTOLOGISTS** announced the **DISCOVERY** of a **15-MILLION-YEAR-OLD FOSSIL** of an extinct species of **BANDICOOT.** They named it *Crash bandicoot* after a **VIDEO GAME CHARACTER.** In the game, **CRASH** is a **MUTANT** bandicoot that can **SPIN** at extreme **SPEED** to knock **ENEMIES** out of the **WAY.**

SOUTHERN BROWN BANDICOOT

BANDI-COOT

If you live in Australia, you might wake up one morning to find your lawn covered in cone-shaped holes. That means a bandicoot has been visiting! These creatures are known as the gardener's best friend because they dig for and eat insects that can destroy homes and gardens, including beetles, termites, and ants.

Bandicoots are small marsupials with long, pointed snouts. They can be as small as a mouse or up to the size of a cat. Bandicoots live all throughout Australia. They look a bit like a cross between a rat and a rabbit, with short, rounded ears and strong hind legs adapted for hopping. They are solitary, nocturnal animals that emerge only at night to search for food. In the dark, they use their excellent senses of smell and hearing to locate plants and insects in the soil.

One group of bandicoots, the rabbit-eared bandicoots, are more commonly known as bilbies. The greater bilby has ears that resemble a rabbit's, and unlike other bandicoots, it burrows underground. Conservationists sometimes call it the "Easter Bilby," Australia's own version of the Easter Bunny. They hope to bring awareness to this vulnerable species, which has lived in Australia for millions of years and is now rarely seen.

Bandicoots, including bilbies, play an important role in their homeland of Australia. When they dig for insects, they turn over soil, helping nutrients cycle through the ground. And bilbies' burrows, which are as deep as seven feet (2.1 m) and shaped like spirals, provide homes for at least 45 different animals, including the venomous king brown snake. A single bilby can dig multiple burrows in a day. That's a lot of houses for Australia's animals!

FACTS

SCIENTIFIC NAME Peramelidae (family)

GROUP NAME None

SIZE Up to 31 inches (80 cm) with a 12-inch (30-cm) tail

WEIGHT Up to 4.4 pounds (2 kg)

EATS Earthworms, spiders, beetles, bulbs, seeds

BILBIES, a type of bandicoot, **LIVE** in parts of the **AUSTRALIAN OUTBACK**, or remote interior of the continent, where **TEMPERATURES** can **REACH 104°F** (40°C).

UP IN THE AIR

WHOOSH! A small, furry figure zooms by, swooping through the forest canopy. It's a glider, a mammal that uses flaps of skin that stretch from wrist to ankle to turn itself into a fur-covered kite. About 15 million years ago, when Australia was covered with a lush rainforest, gliders' unusual way of moving allowed them to take shortcuts from treetop to treetop.

SUGAR GLIDER

It's no bigger than the palm of your hand, but when airborne, the sugar glider can cover half the length of a soccer field. The most common of all Australia's gliders, these critters inhabit the tropical and temperate forests of Australia as well as Indonesia and New Guinea. When gliding, they unfurl membranes that stretch between their fifth forefingers and their back ankles, and they use their bushy tails to control their flight path.

FEATHERTAIL GLIDER

The smallest gliding marsupial in the world, the feathertail glider only grows as big as a small mouse. It's named for its unusual tail, which has stiff, sideways-growing hairs that make it resemble a feather. Feathertail gliders are social animals that live in groups of up to 20. To make a cozy home, they line tree hollows with soft nesting material and curl up together to snooze.

YELLOW-BELLIED GLIDER

Australian campers sometimes describe hearing a strange call in the night: a loud shriek followed by a gurgle. It's no creepy predator, just the call of the yellow-bellied glider. This at-risk species lives in tall eucalyptus forests, often traveling up to 1.2 miles (2 km) away from its treetop den to find food. Its odd noises help it communicate with other gliders in the forest—and also help scare away predators such as foxes and owls.

GREATER GLIDER

This fluffy creature, about the size of a cat, makes its home in tree trunk dens. It can have up to 20 residences, and it's constantly gliding through the forest to move from one to the next. The greater glider is an aerial expert that can glide 328 feet (100 m) in a single swoop—about the length of a major league soccer field! But when it's on the ground, its "wing" flaps just get in the way, earning this animal the reputation as one of the clumsiest gliders in the world.

MAHOGANY GLIDER

The mahogany glider was first described by scientists in 1883. But since it's nocturnal, shy, and nearly silent, it wasn't spotted again for more than 100 years. Experts thought it might have gone extinct, until they finally spotted some in the wild in the northern part of the state of Queensland in 1989. These gliders get their name from their butter-colored bellies. They feed on nectar, pollen, sap, and also honeydew, a sticky liquid that oozes from some insects, such as aphids.

COMMON WOMBAT

FACTS

SCIENTIFIC NAME *Vombatus ursinus*

GROUP NAME Wisdom, mob, colony

SIZE Up to 3.9 feet (1.2 m)

WEIGHT Up to 80 pounds (36 kg)

EATS Grasses, roots, shoots, bark

A wombat's pouch is upside down. Whereas most marsupials' pouches open toward their face, the wombat's opens toward its rear. That's because wombats spend much of their time digging. If a wombat's pouch faced the standard direction, it would fill up with dirt!

Wombats look a bit like small bears, but they really are marsupials. They live in intricate burrows, which have many tunnels and separate areas for sleeping. The tunnels in a wombat burrow can be nearly the length of two football fields at 650 feet (200 m). And some wombats have several burrows that they rotate between depending on the season.

Wombats are built for digging. Using their strong feet and large claws, they can move up to three feet (1 m) of dirt for a tunnel in a single night. They use their burrows for protection against predators such as dingoes and Tasmanian devils.

When threatened, a wombat will sprint toward one of its burrow's entrances at up to 25 miles an hour (40 km/h) and then dive headfirst into the hole. They block the entrance with their rears, which are covered in extra-thick skin. A bite to their backside usually doesn't hurt them!

Wombats survive on a diet of tough plant material such as bark and roots. They have special substances in their stomachs that help break down all that roughage. But the process takes time—a wombat can take about two weeks to digest a meal. And when it comes out the other end, it's in the form of one of the planet's most distinctive droppings: Wombat poo is cube-shaped!

Ancient **ABORIGINAL ROCK ART DEPICTING WOMBATS** dates back 4,000 years.

That's **Fact-tastic!**

BARE-NOSED WOMBATS, a related species, live about **15 YEARS** in the **WILD.** In captivity, they can live longer. One, named **PATRICK THE WOMBAT,** was rescued as an orphan and **LIVED TO AGE 32** at Ballarat Wildlife Park in Victoria, Australia. He was **KNOWN AS** the park's **"WOMBASSADOR."**

COMMON WOMBAT

Opossums will **EAT** almost **ANYTHING**—including **GARBAGE!** That makes some people consider them a nuisance. But opossums also provide **PEST CONTROL** by **EATING MICE, RATS, COCKROACHES, SNAILS,** and **SLUGS.** And they can **DIGEST** almost anything, including a **DEAD ANIMAL'S BONES.**

VIRGINIA OPOSSUM

The opossum lies motionless on the ground, its eyes open and its tongue hanging out. It appears to be dead—but it's all a trick. The animal is just pretending, possibly to fool potential predators into leaving it alone in favor of a fresher meal. This tactic is sometimes called "playing possum."

The Virginia opossum, also called the common opossum, is the only marsupial found north of Mexico. About the size of a large house cat, it has a head shaped like a triangle with a long, pointed nose. Its ears, feet, and tail are hairless. Like some monkeys, opossums have prehensile, or grasping, tails. Their tails can curl around tree branches and even grab and carry objects. And while cartoons often depict opossums snoozing while hanging upside down by their tails, they don't really sleep that way. Only juvenile opossums can hang by their tails for longer than a moment—adults are too heavy!

Like other marsupials, opossums have pouches that they carry their young in. Once the baby opossums get big enough, they move out of the pouch and climb on their mother's back, where they cling tightly to her fur. Juvenile opossums can spend most of their first six weeks of life this way.

Opossums are adaptable animals. The Virginia opossum has made its home in much of North America, living in forests, farmland, and swamps. It eats just about anything, from fruit to insects and even roadkill. If an opossum is threatened, it has many survival strategies it can deploy—it growls, belches, and even poops to discourage something from eating it. And if that doesn't work, it can always play possum!

FACTS

SCIENTIFIC NAME *Didelphis virginiana*

GROUP NAME Passel

SIZE About 30 inches (75 cm) from nose to tail

WEIGHT Up to 13 pounds (6 kg)

EATS Fruit, insects, small mammals, carrion, garbage

Opossums have **OPPOSABLE HALLUCES**—like thumbs, but on their feet **WHERE BIG TOES** would be.

OTHER OPOSSUMS

When many people think of opossums, they think of the Virginia opossum. But there are actually several dozen species of opossum on Earth. And except for the Virginia opossum, which is found in North America, they all crawl and scurry in Mexico, Central America, and South America.

GRAY FOUR-EYED OPOSSUM

This creature is named for the white spots above each eye that make it appear to have four eyes. The gray four-eyed opossum lives from Mexico to northern South America, where it forages for a variety of foods, including fruit, birds, small mammals, and carrion. Unlike other opossums, the gray four-eyed opossum does not "play dead" when threatened. Instead, it opens its mouth wide and hisses loudly as a warning before fighting back.

MOUSE OPOSSUM

There are more than 55 species of mouse opossum, making them the largest opossum family of all. Mouse opossums are skilled climbers, often building their nests in trees and cacti. They can give birth to up to 15 young, but, although they are marsupials, they don't have pouches. Like a mouse, they have nearly naked tails. One species, the fat-tailed mouse opossum, can store fat in its tail to help it survive times when food is scarce.

YAPOK

It's the world's only aquatic, or water-dwelling, marsupial. Also called the water opossum, the yapok lives in freshwater streams and ponds from Mexico to Argentina. It eats fish, crabs, frogs, shrimp, and other small animals that live in and around water. It has webbed hind feet that help it swim and water-repellent fur. But its strangest feature is its pouch, which can seal shut to keep its young dry while it's swimming.

MONITO DEL MONTE

Its name means "little mountain monkey," but it's actually the only living member of a group of marsupials called Micro-biotheria. Scientists believe it is more closely related to the marsupials of Australia than to the ones that share its South American home. About the size of a mouse, the monito del monte has round ears and black rings around its eyes.

WOOLLY OPOSSUM

This group of opossums gets their name from their fluffy tail. They are mostly nocturnal animals that pass the day snoozing in nests they build out of leaves. Rarely found on the ground, they are good climbers that spend nearly their whole lives in the trees. As they move from tree to tree, feasting on fruit, flowers, and small animals, they help pollinate forest plants.

That's
Fact-tastic!

An early **DUTCH VISITOR NAMED** the quokkas' island *RATTENNEST*—Dutch for "rat's nest"—because he **MISTOOK** the **QUOKKAS** for **RATS.** Later, the name became "Rottnest." Small **GROUPS** of **QUOKKAS** also live on **MAINLAND AUSTRALIA.**

QUOKKA

Say cheese! These animals are famous for smiling in photographs. They're quokkas (KWAA-kuhs): furry, teddy-bear-size marsupials that are the only mammal on Rottnest Island off the coast of western Australia. Quokkas are best known for their unusually shaped mouths, which make them appear to have a perpetual grin.

Until 2012, most people outside of Australia had never heard of the quokka. But all that changed when social media was suddenly swamped with quokka selfies—photos tourists take with these smiling critters. Today, Rottnest Island has many visitors, all hoping to snap a pic with a quokka. The quokkas don't seem to mind posing for pictures, and experts say the practice won't harm the animals, as long as tourists keep their hands to themselves. And the grass grown in new areas built to accommodate tourists, as well as the crumbs tourists drop, have given the quokkas a new food source. Their population, which had been in trouble, is now thriving.

When explorers first spotted these fuzzy critters in the late 1600s, they thought the quokkas were rats. But like so many other Australian mammals, quokkas are marsupials related to kangaroos and wallabies. Unlike those creatures, though, quokkas can climb a short distance up trees to reach tasty leaves. Normally nocturnal, the quokkas of Rottnest Island have altered their lifestyle to be awake when the tourists are visiting.

When food is scarce, they can survive for long periods of time without food or water by living on the fat they store in their tails. When food is plentiful, quokkas divide their time between chewing on plants and snoozing in shady spots ... that is, when they're not smiling for a selfie!

FACTS

SCIENTIFIC NAME *Setonix brachyurus*

GROUP NAME Colony

SIZE Up to 35 inches (90 cm)

WEIGHT Up to 9 pounds (4 kg)

EATS Leaves, stems, bark, grass

Quokkas have **TWO STOMACHS.**

EXTINCT POUCHED
MAMMALS

About one million years ago, huge creatures roamed every corner of Earth. This was the age of the enormous mammal. Just as it is today, Australia was home to all kinds of marsupials—only then, they were supersize. Meet some of the monster marsupials of the past.

THYLACINE

Most of Australia's giant animals, also called megafauna, went extinct just tens of thousands of years ago. But not the thylacine *(Thylacinus cynocephalus)*, sometimes called the Tasmanian tiger. The last of these marsupials, which looked a bit like striped wolves, died in 1936—so recently that there is video footage of them. In fact, some people are convinced that a few thylacines still roam the island of Tasmania. But no one has yet managed to prove it.

MARSUPIAL LION

This giant carnivore, *Thylacoleo carnifex,* wielded a set of oversize teeth that may have given it the strongest bite of any mammal predator, living or dead. Though it resembled a modern lion, it was—of course—a marsupial. Instead of using canine teeth for killing, it sported sharp, oversize incisors that delivered a fatal blow to its victims. It also had a stiff, muscular tail that it could use as a tripod while eating or climbing, just like kangaroos do today.

SHORT-FACED KANGAROO

It was the biggest kangaroo to ever hop on planet Earth. The giant short-faced kangaroo, also called *Procoptodon goliah,* stood 6.5 feet (2 m) tall and weighed up to 440 pounds (200 kg), about as much as a full-grown male lion. It had just one oversize toe on each foot and a shortened face, which included its powerful jaws able to bite through branches and other tough food.

PALORCHESTES

Experts once thought that *Palorchestes azael* was a giant kangaroo—even constructing a model of one that resembled a 10-foot (3-m)-tall kangaroo for the Australian Museum in the 1950s. But new discoveries revealed that, unlike a kangaroo, this animal had a small trunk, a bit like a tapir (p. 80). It probably also had a long, grasping tongue that it used to strip leaves off branches, as well as large claws perfect for digging out roots and tubers.

GIANT WOMBAT

The largest marsupial known to have ever lived, the giant wombat, or *Diprotodon optatum,* still roamed across Australia when the first humans arrived there about 65,000 years ago. People lived side by side with this enormous marsupial for more than 20,000 years until *Diprotodon* went extinct. Giant wombats were up to 12 feet (4 m) long and weighed perhaps about three tons (2.7 t)—and gained all that bulk on a diet of plants.

CHAPTER **FIVE**

TOOTHY
MAMMALS

RODENTS

ALL ABOUT RODENTS

On every continent except Antarctica, vast numbers of them wiggle their whiskers and scamper across the ground. They nibble and chew. They are the largest group of mammals on Earth, making up nearly half the species. They are the rodents.

All rodents have powerful jaws and long front teeth that never stop growing their entire lives. These upper and lower front teeth, called incisors, are specially adapted for gnawing. The front side of these teeth is covered with a thick protective coating called enamel. The back side has no enamel. As rodents bite, the back side of their teeth is worn away. This keeps the edges of their teeth super sharp!

Rodents can range in size from the capybara, which is a bit smaller than a full-grown pig, to the tiny mouse, which weighs just about as much as four quarters. They also have a range of lifestyles: While many are herbivores, some are omnivores, and still others are carnivores that prey on insects. Some, like gophers, burrow underground. Others, such as squirrels, live in trees. Rodents can live alone or in large colonies. This order of mammals, called Rodentia, has lived on planet Earth for at least 56 million years. And when modern humans arrived a few hundred thousand years ago, their crops and scraps became a new food source for many rodents. Some of these animals—such as the house mouse—have been alongside people ever since.

PATAGONIAN MARA

SCIENTIFIC NAME: *Dolichotis patagonum*
SIZE: About 28 inches (71 cm)
WEIGHT: About 18 pounds (8 kg)
EATS: Grasses, cacti, other plants

KOZLOV'S PYGMY JERBOA

SCIENTIFIC NAME: *Salpingotus kozlovi*
SIZE: About 2 inches (5 cm) with a tail about 5 inches (13 cm) long
WEIGHT: About 0.3 ounce (9 g)
EATS: Seeds, plants, spiders, insects

CAPE PORCUPINE

SCIENTIFIC NAME: *Hystrix africaeaustralis*

SIZE: Up to 3 feet (0.9 m)

WEIGHT: Up to 65 pounds (30 kg)

EATS: Leaves, roots, tubers, bulbs

MUSKRAT

SCIENTIFIC NAME: *Ondatra zibethicus*

SIZE: Up to 24 inches (61 cm)

WEIGHT: About 2.5 pounds (1.1 kg)

EATS: Plants

NUTRIA

SCIENTIFIC NAME: *Myocastor coypus*

SIZE: Up to 25 inches (64 cm) with a 15-inch (38-cm) tail

WEIGHT: Up to 22 pounds (10 kg)

EATS: Plants

143

MEERKAT

FACTS

SCIENTIFIC NAME *Suricata suricatta*

GROUP NAME Mob

SIZE Up to 14 inches (35 cm) with a tail up to 10 inches (25 cm) long

WEIGHT Up to 2.2 pounds (1 kg)

EATS Insects, lizards, birds, fruit

Several meerkat **"BABYSITTERS"** will stay behind to **WATCH THE YOUNG** while the rest of the mob is out foraging. Different **MEMBERS** of the mob will **TAKE TURNS** babysitting. It's a tough job—**OFTEN**, a meerkat babysitter will **GO** all day **WITHOUT EATING.**

A meerkat stands atop a rock on its hind legs, its head held high. As it scans the horizon for danger, it lets out a series of low peeps—a signal to its fellow meerkats that no threats are in sight. Meerkats take turns standing guard while the others in their group, called a mob, look for food.

When the guard spots a predator, it barks or whistles, using different calls to sound the alarm for enemies coming from the land and enemies coming from the air. All the meerkats bolt for the nearest hole and dive inside for safety. Sometimes, a mob of meerkats will scratch at the ground to create a dust cloud for additional cover. At other times, the whole mob will stand together to look like a big, fierce creature and scare off their opponent. They can even chase off attackers many times their own size.

Meerkats are a member of the mongoose family. They live in the hot, dry environment of southern Africa's Kalahari Desert. Dark patches around their eyes help reduce the sun's glare, and dark skin on their stomachs helps them control their body temperature. Though meerkats are endothermic, or warm-blooded, they use their environment to help adjust their body temperature, a bit like reptiles do. When meerkats want to raise their temperature, they lie on their backs and let the sun's rays warm their bellies. When they want to lower their temperature, they lie stomach-down on a cool rock.

Meerkats live underground in burrows with up to 40 other individuals. Though they are skilled diggers, they prefer to make their homes in burrows dug by other animals, such as ground squirrels. Their burrows can have up to 15 entrance and exit holes and are complete with separate bedrooms and bathrooms. Nice digs!

That's Fact-tastic!

SNAKES often slither their way THROUGH BURROWS on the hunt for a tasty MEERKAT MEAL. So when meerkats see a snake, they go on the ATTACK. A MOB WILL SWARM the snake and BITE IT until the snake gives up and retreats.

That's
Fact-tastic!

A beaver's large,
FLAT TAIL acts like a
BOAT RUDDER. It helps
the beaver **TURN** in the
water as it **PUSHES LOGS**
to make its **DAM.**

AMERICAN BEAVER

What looks like a pile of sticks blocks the flow of a stream, pooling the water into a still pond. But it's no random heap—it's actually a beaver dam. Beavers are nature's construction experts. They use their powerful teeth to gnaw down trees. Then they weave together logs and branches and pack them with mud. This activity turns fields into the large ponds where beavers like to live.

Beavers also build dome-shaped homes, called lodges, out of branches and mud. They often build their lodges in the middle of their ponds to keep them safe from predator attacks. Beaver lodges have entrances that can be reached only from underwater. A whole family, or colony, of beavers will live in the lodge: the beaver parents, their babies, and juvenile beavers born the year before.

Beavers emerge from their lodges at night to build and to eat. They use trees not just as construction materials but also as food. Unlike most other mammals, beavers are able to digest the tough material called cellulose that makes tree trunks strong.

These animals can dramatically transform the places where they live. Beaver dams change the flow of rivers and can flood hundreds of acres. The ponds they form also help filter the water, which keeps it clean. Algae grows in the sunny, still pond water, creating a food source for tiny microscopic organisms. They in turn become food for insects, which become food for all kinds of species, from birds to fish to amphibians. No wonder beavers are sometimes called "ecosystem engineers"!

FACTS

SCIENTIFIC NAME *Castor canadensis*

GROUP NAME Colony

SIZE Up to 39 inches (99 cm) with a tail up to 12 inches (30 cm) long

WEIGHT About 60 pounds (27 kg)

EATS Leaves, bark, twigs, aquatic plants

Beavers can stay **UNDERWATER** for around **15 MINUTES** at a time.

CAPYBARA

It may not look like a mouse or a rat, but the capybara is a rodent—the largest one in the world! Capybaras (ka-puh-BAA-ruhs) stand two feet (60 cm) tall at the shoulder and can weigh up to 145 pounds (66 kg). They look a bit like hairy pigs without a snout, and people once thought they were related to pigs. But capybara's closest relatives are actually guinea pigs (p. 155).

Capybaras are found in Central and South America. They are semiaquatic animals that must live near water because their skin will dry out without frequent swims. They are often found on riverbanks, beside ponds, and in marshes. Capybaras have slightly webbed feet and are excellent swimmers. Like hippos (p. 88), they have small eyes and noses located high on their heads so that they can keep their faces out of the water when they're swimming.

Also like hippos, capybaras often spend the heat of the day wallowing in shallow water and mud to keep cool. At night, they leave the water to graze. Capybaras feed mostly on water plants and grasses, though they'll eat melons and squash if they get the chance. But they do have one strange eating habit: Capybaras begin each morning by snacking on their own poop! Because grasses are hard to digest, this behavior helps them get as many nutrients as they can.

Capybaras are constantly on the alert for predators. That's because jaguars, pumas, and alligator-like animals called caimans all consider the capybara a tasty meal. And young capybaras are in danger from animals such as boa constrictors and birds of prey, too. In areas where most predators hunt at night, capybaras will change their habits to be most active during the day.

In a **NATIVE LANGUAGE** of the **AMAZON**, the capybara is called *kapiyva*, or **"MASTER OF THE GRASSES."**

That's **Fact-tastic!**

Capybaras aren't related to cows. But, **LIKE COWS, THEY REGURGITATE THEIR FOOD,** or vomit it up to chew it again. Also **LIKE COWS, THEY CHEW IN A SIDE-TO-SIDE MOTION,** rather than up-and-down like humans do. These behaviors help them **BREAK DOWN** the **TOUGH PLANTS** and **GRASSES** that make up most of **THEIR DIET.**

149

AIRBORNE
RODENTS

Most squirrels can climb trees—but a few can glide through the air! There are about 50 species of flying squirrels in North and Central America and Southeast and northern Asia. When they leap into a glide, they stretch out their limbs, unfurling a fur-covered membrane called the patagium (pa-TAY-gee-um) that stretches from their wrists to their ankles. They can turn by lowering an arm and can even flip up their fluffy tails to slow down.

SOUTHERN FLYING SQUIRREL

Though southern flying squirrels live from southeastern Canada and as far south as Mexico and Honduras, not many people have seen one in the wild. They may actually be one of the most common mammals never seen by most humans. That's because, like other flying squirrels, they are nocturnal. In fact, many flying squirrels glow bright pink under ultraviolet light—possibly to help them see and communicate with each other in dim conditions.

WOOLLY FLYING SQUIRREL

One of the world's largest flying squirrels, the woolly flying squirrel, can be two feet (0.6 m) tall, with a two-foot (0.6-m) tail. These giant gliders are covered with silky fur and have strange teeth, which they use to eat almost nothing but pine needles. They also have unusual calls that are said to sound like a child screaming. Once thought to be extinct, the woolly flying squirrel was rediscovered in northern Pakistan in 1994.

HUMBOLDT'S FLYING SQUIRREL

Until 2017, scientists thought there were only two species of flying squirrel—northern and southern—in North America. But then biologists realized that the squirrels of the Pacific Northwest were actually a separate species. These palm-size, dark-colored critters glide through the moss-covered forests of that region. They can soar 150 feet (46 m) in a single glide and land with extreme accuracy.

SCALY-TAILED SQUIRRELS

There are seven species in this family of mostly gliding, fluffy-tailed creatures, and they all live in the forests of Central Africa. But though they resemble flying squirrels, they belong to a totally separate branch of the rodent family tree. They have skulls and teeth adapted for eating tough bark, large guts for digesting this tough food, and tails that are scaly at the base. They also have bony growths on their elbows that they use to extend their gliding membranes for extra distance and control.

HOSE'S PYGMY FLYING SQUIRREL

It's the smallest flying squirrel in the world: At about three ounces (85 g), a Hose's pygmy flying squirrel weighs less than a deck of cards. It can be found only in a small area of the northwestern side of the island of Borneo. These flying squirrels live almost entirely in the trees, gliding from one to the other and using holes in the trunks to make their nests.

NAKED MOLE RAT

FACTS

SCIENTIFIC NAME *Heterocephalus glaber*

GROUP NAME Colony

SIZE Up to 7 inches (17 cm) with a 3-inch (7.6-cm) tail

WEIGHT Up to 1.2 oz (35 g)

EATS Roots, tubers

If the naked mole rat QUEEN DIES, FEMALES will sometimes FIGHT TO THE DEATH to become the NEW QUEEN.

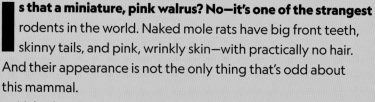

Is that a miniature, pink walrus? No—it's one of the strangest rodents in the world. Naked mole rats have big front teeth, skinny tails, and pink, wrinkly skin—with practically no hair. And their appearance is not the only thing that's odd about this mammal.

Naked mole rats live in the deserts of eastern Africa, where daytime temperatures can soar. To escape the heat, naked mole rats live underground—so they don't need hair for sun protection. And if they get chilly, they huddle together in a pile— so they don't need hair to keep warm. But naked mole rats aren't completely hairless: About 100 hairs do poke out of their bodies, which the naked mole rats use like whiskers to help them feel their way around their tunnels. They also have hair between their toes that they use to help brush the soil behind themselves while digging.

Most mole rats are solitary animals. But not naked mole rats. These animals live in very unusual groups. They are one of only two mammals (the other is another kind of mole rat) that live a eusocial (yew-SO-shul) lifestyle. That means their groups are led by a dominant female called the queen that is the only one in the group to breed and give birth. The digging of burrows and gathering of food is done by worker mole rats. Other mole rats take care of the queen. In this way, naked mole rats are more similar to ants or bees than they are to other mammals.

The underground home of a naked mole rat colony is impressive. It contains a nursery where the queen mole rat resides along with her babies. It has pantries where food is stored. It even has a bathroom! A naked mole rat burrow can house as many as 300 individuals. All together, its tunnels can total 2.5 miles (4 km) and cover the area of six football fields.

That's **Fact-tastic!**

With a **LIFE SPAN** of about **30 YEARS,** naked mole rats are the **LONGEST-LIVING RODENTS** known. They experience **REMARKABLY GOOD HEALTH** (they rarely get cancer) and are **UNUSUALLY HEARTY** (they can survive for up to 18 minutes without oxygen). Strangest of all, they also don't appear to age: One 2018 study found that as **MOLE RATS GET OLDER,** their **RISK OF DEATH DOES NOT INCREASE,** as it does for every other known mammal.

PET RODENTS

Not all rodents wiggle their whiskers in the wild—some are kept as pets. Here are six rodent species that have been domesticated for human companionship. They may be a more unusual choice than a dog or cat, but rodents can make excellent buddies for people all the same.

FANCY MOUSE

Fancy mice are simply domesticated versions of the house mice that live in basements and attics. Pet mice can be more skittish than other small rodents. But with lots of gentle care and treats, they can learn to be held and to take treats from their owner's hand. Mice are active and curious, so they need an enclosure that gives them space to tunnel, nest, and chew. They are also nocturnal animals, making them good pets for people who are gone all day and home at night.

SYRIAN HAMSTER

Also known as the golden hamster, this rodent originally comes from the deserts of northern Syria and southern Turkey. In the wild, Syrian hamsters are highly territorial, and as pets, they are only comfortable living alone or they will fight with each other. Hamsters are nocturnal, and they will stay up at night burrowing, playing, and chewing.

GUINEA PIG

Guinea pigs, also called cavies, were once wild animals that lived in the forests, savannas, grasslands, and mountains of South America. But more than 3,000 years ago, the Inca domesticated guinea pigs to be both food and pets. Guinea pigs thrive when kept in pairs or groups. When happy, they show it by "popcorning," or jumping high in the air.

Animals should NEVER BE TAKEN FROM THE WILD, so be sure to research where your potential pet came from. SOME SPECIES ARE ILLEGALLY CAUGHT and then sold or bred in crowded and unsafe conditions.

CHINCHILLA

These animals are best known for their incredibly soft, thick fur. In their wild home of South American mountains, this fur helps keep them warm. In captivity, it may cause them to overheat, so pet chinchillas need a cool spot in the house. Chinchillas are shy creatures that sometimes never learn to be held. But with regular training, they can become attached to their owners.

FANCY RAT

They're not the same as the creatures that scurry down the subway tracks or in the walls of your house. Rats bred to be pets, called fancy rats, can make surprisingly good companions. While some pet rodents can be skittish or even aggressive, rats are often friendly and curious, and like to cuddle. Studies even suggest that rats dream when they sleep and giggle when tickled—the sound is just too high-pitched for humans to hear!

MONGOLIAN GERBIL

In the wild, these furry critters inhabit the semideserts and steppes of Mongolia, where they spend much of their time in underground burrows. They are highly social animals that live in colonies. That means that if given regular handling, they can become tame pets with gentle temperaments. Because they are social, gerbils do best when kept with another gerbil.

Some mammals, such as
MONKEYS and **HUMANS,**
SWEAT to **COOL DOWN.** Others,
such as **DOGS, PANT.** But unlike
their mammal cousins,
KANGAROO RATS DON'T
DO EITHER. This **HELPS** their
bodies **CONSERVE WATER,**
a scarce resource in
their **DESERT HOME.**

KANGAROO RAT

In the deserts of the American West, tiny rodents fight off rattlesnakes in life-and-death battles. The combat takes place in complete darkness. And it usually lasts only about 50 milliseconds—at least twice the speed of the blink of an eye. But in that time, kangaroo rats become tiny ninjas, kicking, rolling, and leaping as high as eight feet (2.4 m) in the air to fend off their foes.

They aren't related to the Australian marsupials (p. 112), but they do hop along on their hind legs, just like kangaroos. These rodents may resemble rats at first glance—but they have oversize hind feet and exceptionally long tails with a tuft at the end.

Kangaroo rats live in desert environments of western North America, from southern Canada to Mexico. But most people who inhabit this region have never seen one. That's because they are shy animals that are only active at night. Then they come out of their cool burrows to forage for seeds, which they carry in pouches in their cheeks and store in their burrows. Kangaroo rats are able to get all the water they need from their seed diet and can go their whole lives without ever drinking any water.

Though they have many predators, including owls and bobcats, kangaroo rats are remarkably skilled at fighting back against one particular foe: sidewinder rattlesnakes. First, the kangaroo rat will try to deter an attacking snake by showing off its strength and speed. It will drum its feet on the ground, jump in the air, and kick sand at its predator. If the snake strikes, the kangaroo rat uses incredible agility to dodge its fangs. In one 2017 study, scientists observed 23 of these desert duels with night vision cameras. The kangaroo rats were able to outwit the snakes every time.

FACTS

SCIENTIFIC NAME	*Dipodomys* (genus)
GROUP NAME	None
SIZE	Up to 8 inches (20 cm) with an 8-inch (20-cm) tail
WEIGHT	Up to 6 ounces (170 grams)
EATS	Seeds

Kangaroo rats have such **GOOD HEARING** that they **CAN DETECT** a nearly **SILENT OWL** flying by.

RODENTS
IN YOUR BACKYARD

About 15,000 years ago, ancient humans began to change their lifestyle. Instead of living life on the move, hunting and gathering their food from the wild, they became farmers. And as they made this shift, the house mouse went with them. The more humans settled down, the more mice joined them, attracted by the grains they grew and stored away. These rodents, and others too, still live close by us today.

GROUNDHOG

Most people know the groundhog as an animal that can predict how long winter will last. While that's just a silly story, it has a basis in truth: If you spot a wild groundhog out and about during winter months, it can signal that the season may be coming to an end. That's because groundhogs, also called woodchucks, hibernate. As they rest the winter away in their dens, their heart slows to just five beats per minute and they breathe just twice per minute. Their body temperature drops to as low as 37°F (2.8°C).

PRAIRIE DOG

While prairie dogs forage for grasses, roots, and seeds, a few members of the group always stand guard, acting as lookouts. When a threat is spotted, the lookout will cry out, alerting the group to retreat to the burrow. There are five different species of prairie dogs—which are another type of squirrel. They live in extensive burrows on North America's prairies and grasslands. One prairie dog "town" covered 25,000 square miles (64,750 sq km) and was home to about four million prairie dogs!

SQUIRREL

Visit a park nearly anywhere in the world and you'll probably spot a squirrel. There are more than 200 species of these whisker-twitching, fluffy-tailed critters, and they live everywhere except Australia. They can be tiny (the African pygmy squirrel is just five inches [13 cm] long) or large (the Indian giant squirrel can reach three feet [1 m]). Some live in trees and spend their days leaping from branch to branch, whereas others live on the ground and shelter in burrows and tunnels.

CHIPMUNK

These striped, bushy-tailed critters resemble squirrels—and that's because chipmunks are actually a type of squirrel. They are small critters that weigh between one and five ounces (28–125 g). When food is plentiful, chipmunks spend much of their time collecting it and storing it for later: A single chipmunk can gather up to 165 acorns in a single day! They use their oversize cheek pouches—which can stretch to three times the size of their head—to hold that large load.

HOUSE MOUSE

They're the same species as the "fancy mouse" (p. 154) commonly kept as pets—but that doesn't mean you can bring a wild mouse into your house as a pet! Native to Eurasia, this mammal has migrated alongside humans to live everywhere people do. It can survive nearly everywhere from cornfields to on board ships. House mice are agile animals that can climb, jump, and even swim. They eat insects, seeds, or just about anything else they find. It's no wonder they can be found in nearly every corner of the world!

AGOUTI

FACTS

SCIENTIFIC NAME *Dasyprocta* (genus)

GROUP NAME None

SIZE Up to 30 inches (76 cm)

WEIGHT Up to 13 pounds (6 kg)

EATS Seeds

Agoutis are **RELATED** to **GUINEA PIGS** and **CHINCHILLAS.**

It might look a little like an oversize gerbil, but this is no pet. The agouti is a wild creature native to the rainforests of Central and South America. It has glossy brown fur, sports a tiny bump of a tail, and moves through the forest like a ballerina, by walking on its tiptoes.

Many predators lurk in the shadows of the rainforest, including jaguars and ocelots. That has made the agouti an expert at evasion. When it's not looking for food, the agouti spends much of its time hiding in a burrow or hollow tree trunk. It uses its excellent senses of smell and hearing to keep on the alert for potential attackers. If one gets too close, the agouti will stamp its feet, call out, or raise the hairs on its rump to try to scare off the animal. If that doesn't work, the agouti will flee, sprinting and jumping up to six feet (1.8 m) straight in the air.

Agoutis play an important role in helping rainforest plants grow. They collect seeds to eat and save the extras for later by burying them throughout their territories. If an agouti buries a seed and doesn't return to retrieve it, that seed might grow into a plant—eventually producing more seeds to feed more agoutis! Agoutis are able to eat seeds too tough for other critters to crack open. They sit on their haunches, holding the seeds in their front paws while they gnaw at them with their strong teeth.

When baby agoutis are born, they are already able to fend for themselves. Early in the morning on their first day of life, a mother of the species known as the Central American agouti shows her young potential nesting sites in the area—often burrows dug by other animals. The young agoutis choose one site and gather leaves and twigs to line their new nest. These nests are too small for predators to enter—and they are too small for the mother to enter, too! Baby agoutis rest and sleep alone. Every morning and evening, they rejoin their mother to feed.

That's Fact-tastic!

The agouti is the ONLY ANIMAL ON EARTH able to CRACK OPEN the tough shell of a BRAZIL NUT. Agoutis get this ability from their unusual teeth: The hard outer covering on their teeth, called ENAMEL, is TWISTED, which gives their TEETH EXTRA STRENGTH.

EXTINCT RODENTS

Rodents burrow, climb, and even glide. They are some of the most adaptable animals on Earth, capable of surviving in nearly every environment, from deserts to wetlands—and even in smelly sewers! The rodents of the past were no different, and their unique adaptations are perhaps even odder than those of their modern relatives.

HORNED GOPHER

It looked like a cross between a groundhog and a rhinoceros. In the history of life on our planet, the horned gopher is the only rodent that has ever been discovered to have evolved horns on its nose. It lived in North America about 10 million years ago. Six species of horned gophers have been discovered so far. Scientists think that the twin horns on their snouts were used for fighting off predators, such as ancient species of badgers, skunks, and hawks.

GIANT BEAVER

In 1891, a rancher in Nebraska, U.S.A., found a strange fossil that baffled experts. It was a 6.5-foot (2-m) corkscrew made of stone. Was it an extinct sponge? The root of a giant tree? Neither. The odd rock was actually the fossilized burrow of a 22-million-year-old beaver named *Palaeocastor*. Experts think these rodents dug their strangely shaped homes because so many beavers lived in the same area at the time—at least 15 species. With little room underground left, *Palaeocastor* found space by digging deep vertical burrows ... sort of like skyscrapers in reverse!

NEOEPIBLEMA ACREENSIS

This rodent was all brawn and no brains. *Neoepiblema acreensis* lived about 10 million years ago in what is now Brazil and, at an estimated 176 pounds (80 kg), was much larger than its modern relative, the chinchilla. When scientists peered into its fossilized skull, they found something surprising—its brain was incredibly small—maybe weighing half as much as a mandarin orange! Scientists think that because it lived before the time of most large predators, it didn't need a big brain to evade them.

RUGOSODON EURASIATICUS

When an asteroid slammed into Earth 66 million years ago, wiping out nearly all of the dinosaurs, the age of mammals began. With many of their predators and competitors for food gone, the mammals that had been quietly living alongside the dinosaurs could now take over. One of them was *Rugosodon eurasiaticus*, a kind of creature called a multituberculate, a branch of the mammal family that is now extinct. These animals weren't rodents, but they played the same role in the ecosystem as modern rodents: climbing trees, digging tunnels, and feasting on leaves, seeds, worms, and insects.

PHOBEROMYS PATTERSONI

The sight of a scurrying mouse is enough to make some people shriek in surprise. But imagine if that mouse stood more than four feet (1.2 m) tall and weighed as much as a horse! This was *Phoberomys pattersoni,* a relative of the guinea pig that lived about eight million years ago. It likely lived like a modern capybara, foraging along riverbanks. But its enormous bulk would have probably made it too big to burrow like most modern rodents do.

CHAPTER **SIX**

OCEANGOING MAMMALS

MARINE MAMMALS

ALL ABOUT MARINE MAMMALS

Like all other mammals, they have hair, bear live young, and breathe air. But unlike other mammals, they aren't land dwellers. Instead, they live in or near the ocean.

The ancestors of all living marine mammals were land animals. But the different groups of modern marine mammals—such as the cetaceans, which includes whales and dolphins, and the pinnipeds, which includes seals—do not share a common ancestor. Instead, each evolved from a different type of land animal. Because of this, modern marine mammals belong to several different family groups: Sea lions, for example, are part of the carnivore family, and sea otters are members of the weasel family. What they have in common is that millions of years ago, their ancestors left the land and entered the sea. Over time, they adapted to their new environment and became able to swim, dive, and hunt underwater. Many even evolved similar traits, such as flipper-like limbs and the ability to store lots of oxygen for deep dives.

Most aquatic animals breathe with gills, which pull oxygen out of the water. Even though many spend nearly their whole lives at sea, marine mammals don't have gills. Instead, they must come to the surface to breathe. And though they don't look furry, even marine mammals such as whales have hair. Some have bumps containing hairs along their chin and jaws. Others have a fuzz of hair before they're born and lose it soon after birth. And, like other mammals, they nurse their young with milk—many just do it underwater!

STEJNEGER'S BEAKED WHALE

SCIENTIFIC NAME: *Mesoplodon stejnegeri*

SIZE: Up to 19 feet (5.8 m)

WEIGHT: More than 3,500 pounds (1,580 kg)

EATS: Squid, fish

HARP SEAL

SCIENTIFIC NAME: *Pagophilus groenlandicus*

SIZE: Up to 6 feet (1.8 m)

WEIGHT: Up to 300 pounds (136 kg)

EATS: Fish, marine invertebrates

HARBOR PORPOISE

SCIENTIFIC NAME: *Phocoena phocoena*

SIZE: Up to 6.5 feet (2 m)

WEIGHT: Up to 170 pounds (77 kg)

EATS: Fish, mollusks

DUGONG

SCIENTIFIC NAME: *Dugong dugon*

SIZE: Up to 13 feet (4 m)

WEIGHT: Up to 880 pounds (400 kg)

EATS: Plants like seagrass, worms, and algae

BLUE WHALE

FACTS

SCIENTIFIC NAME *Balaenoptera musculus*

GROUP NAME Pod

SIZE Up to 105 feet (32 m)

WEIGHT Up to 200 tons (181 t)

EATS Krill

A blue whale's **CALLS** can be **LOUDER** than a **JET ENGINE.**

A **blue whale is more than twice as heavy as a space** shuttle, with a heart that weighs as much as a car and a tongue that weighs as much as an elephant. They are not only the largest animals on Earth, they are also the largest animals ever known to have lived in the history of our planet.

Blue whales reach their gargantuan size by feeding on some of the smallest animals to inhabit the ocean: tiny shrimplike creatures called krill. They eat by gulping an enormous mouthful of krill-filled water. Then they use their huge tongues to push the water out of their mouths, filtering it through fringed plates (called baleen) attached to their upper jaws and leaving the krill behind. During certain times of the year, a single adult blue whale can eat about four tons (3.6 t) a day. That's equivalent to the weight of a hippopotamus!

These massive mammals cruise all the world's oceans except for the Arctic. Each year, they migrate more than 4,000 miles (6,400 km) to travel between their summer feeding grounds in the north and their winter mating grounds in the tropics. Though they usually make their way alone, blue whales do keep in touch with each other. Their songs—some of the loudest sounds of any animal—can travel up to 1,000 miles (1,600 km) through the ocean. Much about these songs remains mysterious.

Like all other mammals, blue whales give birth to live young. From the moment their babies are born, they are already some of the planet's largest animals: They can weigh up to three tons (2.7 t) and be 25 feet (7.6 m) long. That's longer than a full-grown giraffe is tall!

That's
Fact-tastic!

Scientists can tell a **BLUE WHALE'S AGE** by studying the **LAYERS** that make up its **WAXLIKE EARPLUGS**— similar to **COUNTING** the **RINGS** of a **TREE TRUNK!** They have learned that blue whales are some of the **PLANET'S LONGEST-LIVING ANIMALS,** with some reaching about **110 YEARS OLD.**

WHALES OF THE WORLD

Whales swim in every ocean on Earth. All are massive: Even the smallest among them, the dwarf sperm whale, weighs 600 pounds (272 kg)—more than a full-grown pig. Meet some of the planet's most wonderful whales.

SPERM WHALE

The massive head of a sperm whale houses an equally large brain—the largest of any creature ever known to have lived! A sperm whale's head also holds large amounts of a mysterious substance called spermaceti. Researchers don't know what it is used for, though they think it may have something to do with helping whales stay down deep in the water. Sperm whales hunt by diving very deep, where they feast on sharks, fish, and even elusive giant squid.

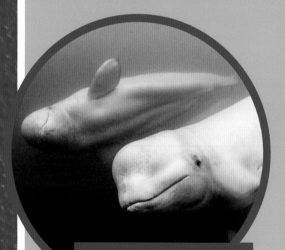

BELUGA WHALE

They are the only entirely white whales in the world. Belugas inhabit the cold waters of the Arctic Ocean but migrate south in large groups when the sea freezes over each winter. The beluga's thick layer of blubber keeps it warm in its chilly habitat. A rounded structure on top of its head, called the melon, helps the whale refine its echolocation signals to better navigate.

GRAY WHALE

Gray whales are some of the planet's most impressive long-distance travelers. Every year, they migrate from Alaska to Mexico, a journey that covers 12,400 miles (20,000 km) round trip! They are curious animals and will often swim up to investigate boats that they encounter during their journeys. That makes gray whales popular among whale-watchers.

HUMPBACK WHALE

Humpback whales are longer than a city bus. But despite their bulk, they are incredible acrobats. Using their huge tail fin, called a fluke, they can power themselves right out of the water, landing with an enormous splash. They're also known to rise vertically above the surface, a behavior called spyhopping.

CUVIER'S BEAKED WHALE

Imagine being able to take a deep breath, plunge underwater, and then stay down for almost four hours. Of course, humans can't even come close to holding their breath for that long, but that's what the Cuvier's beaked whale can do. The deepest-diving mammal on Earth, it can glide nearly 9,850 feet (3,000 m) under the ocean's surface in its search for squid to eat. Males have just two teeth at the tip of their lower jaw, which they use for fighting. They can't grab on to their slippery prey, so instead these whales slurp down the squid like spaghetti!

BOWHEAD WHALE

The bowhead is likely the longest-living mammal on planet Earth. But exactly how old it can get is hard for researchers to say. Some bowhead whales have been discovered with remnants of harpoons dating back to the 1880s embedded in their flesh. Experts estimate that they can live at least 200 years, though they could possibly live as long as 268 years.

That's
Fact-tastic!

Just like humans, bottlenose dolphins **CHOOSE** other **DOLPHINS** to become **BUDDIES** with based on **SHARED INTERESTS.** Scientists have discovered that dolphins that **USE SEA SPONGES** to **PROTECT** their **BEAKS** as they **FORAGE** on the **SEAFLOOR,** a behavior **CALLED** "**SPONGING,**" make **FRIENDS** with **OTHER SPONGERS.** These bonds can last for decades.

BOTTLENOSE DOLPHIN

A **pod of bottlenose dolphins glides through the water,** reaching speeds of 22 miles an hour (35 km/h). They frolic, spin, and leap, jumping out of the water higher than 16 feet (4.9 m). Bottlenose dolphins are some of the planet's most talented acrobats. They're also thought to be some of the most intelligent animals on Earth.

Bottlenose dolphins live in warm waters throughout the world, often preferring areas like harbors, bays, and coastlines that put them close to humans. They are known to even follow fishing boats in the hopes of snapping up some leftovers! This close contact with people means they are easy to view in the wild and has made them one of the best-studied marine mammals on the planet.

Highly social animals, bottlenose dolphins travel in tightly knit groups. They often cooperate with one another when hunting and catching fish. Sometimes, a pod of dolphins will encircle a school of fish and herd the fish into a small ball. Then the dolphins will take turns charging through the ball, eating as many fish as they can grab. Near the surface, dolphins will swim on their sides, circling a school of fish and forcing the fish into a tight group. All at once, the dolphins will turn inward and snap up their meal. In some areas, dolphins even herd schools of fish into sandbars or shorelines to trap them. The dolphins will lunge out of the water to grab the fish.

To track their prey, dolphins use echolocation. They send out a stream of clicking noises—up to 1,000 per second. The noises travel underwater, where they bounce off objects and head back to the dolphin that sent them. From listening to these echoes, dolphins can tell the location, size, and shape of the object—even in dark or murky water. Neat trick!

FACTS

SCIENTIFIC NAME *Tursiops truncatus*

GROUP NAME Pod

SIZE Up to 14 feet (4.3 m)

WEIGHT Up to 1,100 pounds (500 kg)

EATS Fish

BABY DOLPHINS are BORN with HAIRS on their SNOUTS.

CETACEAN COMMUNICATION

A haunting melody booms across the vast ocean—the song of a humpback whale. Moans, cries, and groans weave together, forming a song that can last 35 minutes. Humpback whales don't just sing—they compose. A pod of whales all sing the same song. But as they sing, individuals will make up new parts, and the other whales listen and sing them, too. Over time, the pod's song will change into a whole new tune.

Scientists aren't sure why humpbacks perform their songs, but they think whale songs help the humpbacks find a mate, let other whales know their location, or announce their location as they migrate. What's for sure is that the whales are communicating. While humans rely most strongly on our sense of vision, things are different

SOUND TRAVELS about **FOUR TIMES FASTER UNDERWATER** than it does through **AIR.**

BOTTLENOSE DOLPHINS

ORCAS

HUMPBACK WHALES

in the underwater world, which is often too dark and murky to see well. Cetaceans, the group that includes dolphins and whales, have highly developed hearing systems that they use to listen to one another. Perhaps that's why songs and other vocal communications are so important to them.

Dolphins use echolocation for hunting. But they have a whole different sound system that they use for communication: whistling. Scientists believe that every dolphin has its own unique whistle, and dolphins use these "signature whistles" just like humans use their names. When swimming in a group, dolphins call out each individual's signature whistle to help keep track of all the group's members. Dolphins will also call out a companion's signature whistle to get that dolphin's attention. Pregnant dolphins even sing their own signature whistles over and over to their unborn babies!

What are whales and dolphins saying when they "talk" to each other? Scientists hope that we may be able to find out. Biologist Denise Herzing has been studying dolphins for decades. She created a keyboard with buttons labeled with things dolphins like to play with, such as seaweed and rope. When a researcher pressed the buttons, each one made a unique whistle. Wild dolphins quickly learned to imitate the correct whistle to get the toy they wanted. Herzing thinks that this may be the first step toward learning how dolphin language works. She hopes that someday humans and dolphins will be able to have a conversation!

When ships are near, dolphins use HIGHER FREQUENCY WHISTLES so they can HEAR each other over the ships' SONAR BLIPS.

SEA OTTER

FACTS

SCIENTIFIC NAME *Enhydra lutris*

GROUP NAME Raft

SIZE About 4 feet (1.2 m)

WEIGHT About 65 pounds (29.5 kg)

EATS Shellfish, sea urchins, crabs, fish

A sea otter **PUP'S FUR TRAPS** so much **AIR** that it **CAN'T DIVE UNDERWATER.** If it **TRIES,** it just **POPS BACK UP** to the surface!

Sea otters spend much of their time floating. Gathered in large groups, they eat and even sleep this way. Mothers also care for their babies while floating on their backs, nursing and cuddling them.

Many sea otters live in parts of the ocean called kelp forests. Kelp is a type of seaweed that can grow very tall, from the ocean floor to the water's surface. Sometimes, otters wrap the seaweed around their bodies to keep themselves from drifting away while they snooze.

These mammals are perfectly adapted for life in the water. Along with webbed feet, they have nostrils and ears that close when they move beneath the waves, along with a thick coat of water-repellent fur. Their coats are the thickest and most luxurious of any animal on Earth, with as many as one million hairs per square inch (6.5 sq cm)! A sea otter's coat has two layers: an undercoat of shorter hairs and an outer coat of longer guard hairs. This arrangement helps the coat act like a blanket, trapping a layer of warm air next to the otter's skin to keep the animal warm and dry even in cold water. To make sure their coat stays water-repellent, otters spend a lot of time grooming themselves. After every meal, they use their teeth and paws to clean every speck of food and dirt off themselves.

Otters' coats help these animals survive. But they also nearly led to their extinction. Sea otters once roamed from Mexico to Alaska and all the way to Japan. But the animals were hunted for their fur, and by the early 20th century, less than 2,000 were left. Now sea otters are a protected species, and they are making a slow but steady comeback. Today, there are about 3,000 otters that live off the coast of northern California, with two other populations in Alaska and Russia.

That's Fact-tastic!

Sometimes
CONSERVATIONISTS RESCUE
orphaned **BABY** otters. **CAPTIVE**
FEMALE OTTERS that can't be
released back to nature will
"ADOPT" the **LITTLE OTTERS**
and **RAISE THEM** as their **OWN.**
When the little otters are
STRONG ENOUGH, they
are **RETURNED**
to the **WILD.**

That's
Fact-tastic!

MOTHER walruses are **HIGHLY PROTECTIVE** of their **BABIES.** If her **CALF** is **THREATENED,** a **MOTHER** walrus will **PICK IT UP** with her **FLIPPERS,** hold it to **HER CHEST,** and **DIVE** into the **WATER,** swimming away to **SAFETY.**

WALRUS

The walrus rears out of the water, stabbing its enormous tusks into the Arctic ice. Using them for leverage, it hauls its huge body out of the water. Both male and female walruses have tusks, which are actually elongated canine teeth that can be nearly three feet (1 m) long. Walruses use them to "tooth-walk," as well as to break breathing holes in the ice from below. Male walruses also use them to intimidate and fight off other males.

There are two main families of walrus. Atlantic walruses live near the coasts from northeastern Canada to Greenland. Pacific walruses make their home in the seas of northern Russia and Alaska. Walruses are some of the largest pinnipeds, a group that also includes seals and sea lions. A fully grown male walrus can weigh as much as a midsize car. Much of that bulk is blubber: fat that insulates the walrus' body and allows it to survive in the extreme cold of the waters near the Arctic Circle.

Walruses are extremely social animals that gather by the hundreds to sunbathe on the ice in groups called herds. During mating season, gatherings of walruses can number among the thousands. Females and males separate into their own herds, with each female group watched over by a dominant male walrus. The dominant male is usually the biggest and most aggressive male around, and he will stay in charge unless a bigger, stronger walrus successfully battles him for control of his herd.

A fight between two enormous male walruses is a sight to behold. But most of the time, these animals are the gentle giants of the Arctic. Although they are carnivores, they are not aggressive hunters. Instead, they feed on small creatures like crabs and clams, using their sensitive whiskers to seek out this prey on the ocean floor.

FACTS

SCIENTIFIC NAME *Odobenus rosmarus*

GROUP NAME Herd

SIZE Up to 11.5 feet (3.5 m)

WEIGHT Up to 3,300 pounds (1,300 kg)

EATS Crustaceans, shellfish

Walruses can **LIVE** to be **40 YEARS OLD.**

THE WALKING WHALE

Whales do everything in the water, from feeding to sleeping to giving birth. Yet they are mammals just like dogs and cows, and they must come to the surface to breathe air. Why would an air-breathing animal make its home in the ocean?

Like all other marine mammals, whales didn't start out as ocean creatures. The ancestor of whales was a doglike animal that had four legs and walked on land. Then, more than 50 million years ago, that land-living animal gradually gave up its life on the ground and entered the sea. Experts know this because they have discovered fossils of whale ancestors that have traits of both land-living and ocean-swimming animals. These creatures could be found along coastlines, where they lived a semiaquatic lifestyle like today's sea otters or platypuses. Scientists have nicknamed these creatures "walking whales."

AMBULOCETUS

AMBULOCETUS NATANS FOSSIL

One "walking whale" was *Ambulocetus natans*. It was discovered in what is now northern Pakistan. When this creature lived there, 49 million years ago, the area was covered in shallow seas and rivers. *Ambulocetus* was about 12 feet (3.7 m) long and weighed about 400 pounds (181 kg). It had a mouthful of sharp teeth, flipper-like hind feet, and short legs that splayed out sideways, like a crocodile's. On land, *Ambulocetus* was probably clumsy, waddling and pulling its body along with its front legs. In the water, it was likely a graceful swimmer. Experts think it hunted like a modern crocodile, eating fish in the water and ambushing coastline prey animals that got too close to the water's edge.

On the outside, modern whales don't seem to have any evidence of their old walking lifestyle. But they do carry clues of their land-living past in their bones. X-rays show that tiny remains of hind legs still grow in the skeletons of some whales. These leftover bits show that the ancestor of whales once really did walk our planet.

THE AMAZING FOSSIL FIND IN THE PERUVIAN DESERT

WHEN WHALES SWAM

Ancient whale relatives lived first on land and then along coastlines like modern crocodiles. But when did they start to take to the sea full-time? Scientists got a clue in 2019, when they announced they had discovered a 43-million-year-old fossil of a whale ancestor in Peru. It was about 10 feet (3 m) long and looked a bit like an otter, with four legs and a large tail. Though this animal was still able to walk on land, it could also swim long distances. Similar fossils have been discovered in West Africa, showing that these whale ancestors were able to swim from Asia, where they evolved, to South America, continents which were separated by about 746 miles (1,200 km) at the time. The ancient animals would have been adrift for at least a week, able to sleep in the water and survive without freshwater.

Narwhals usually swim in small groups. But when they **MIGRATE**, they can come **TOGETHER** by the **THOUSANDS**. Though they **NEVER LEAVE ARCTIC WATERS**, they **SPEND** their **SUMMERS** on the **COASTS**. Each **FALL**, these **WATERS** become **COVERED** with **ICE**, so narwhals **MIGRATE** offshore to **ICE-FREE WATERS**.

NARWHAL

Long ago, some kings and queens paid enormous sums for scepters made from unicorn horns—or at least what they *believed* were unicorn horns. Their scepters were actually made from the tusks of narwhals, which are sometimes called the "unicorns of the sea."

Narwhals are considered toothed whales, along with dolphins and orcas. But a narwhal has no teeth inside its mouth. Instead, it has one canine tooth that never grows into its jaw and another that grows right through its upper lip ... and becomes its tusk! On rare occasions, both teeth will grow in, becoming double tusks. Tusks grow in a spiral shape and can be up to 10 feet (3 m) long. Usually only males grow tusks, but sometimes a female narwhal will grow a small one.

Narwhals are elusive animals. That, together with their isolated Arctic home, makes them difficult to study. Much about these animals remains mysterious, including the function of their tusks. Scientists have long wondered what they might be used for. Then, in 2017, drones in the far northeast of Canada captured video footage of narwhals doing something no one had ever seen before: smacking Arctic cod with their tusks to stun them, then gobbling the fish up. Now researchers know narwhals use their tusks for hunting. But they may use them for other activities, too, such as breaking up sea ice or fighting over mates.

Of all the toothed whales, narwhals are among the most skilled divers. They can dive more than a mile (1.6 km) and stay underwater for 25 minutes. During a dive, a narwhal's body redirects oxygen to fuel only its muscles and vital organs. When it finally does need a breath of air, the narwhal will pop up to the surface through cracks in the ice.

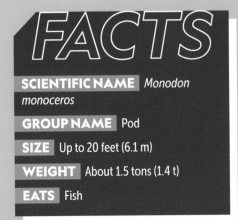

FACTS

SCIENTIFIC NAME *Monodon monoceros*

GROUP NAME Pod

SIZE Up to 20 feet (6.1 m)

WEIGHT About 1.5 tons (1.4 t)

EATS Fish

Narwhals get **LIGHTER** in **COLOR** as they **AGE**. The **OLDEST** narwhals are **NEARLY WHITE.**

ORCA

FACTS

SCIENTIFIC NAME *Orcinus orca*

GROUP NAME Pod

SIZE Up to 32 feet (9.7 m)

WEIGHT Up to 6 tons (5.4 t)

EATS Sea lions, whales, seals

They're sometimes called "killer whales." But orcas are actually the largest member of the dolphin family. At up to 32 feet (9.7 m), an orca can be as long as a school bus! And they are some of the most skillful hunters on the planet.

Orcas inhabit a larger range than any other mammal on Earth, besides humans. Though they are often found in cold northern waters, orcas can live in any climate, from the warm waters near the Equator to the frigid oceans near the poles. They often attack large marine mammals, such as sea lions and whales, but will eat just about any animal they come across, even beaching themselves on land to grab seals and leaping out of the air to snag sea birds.

Though they live in the ocean, orcas' hunting techniques are similar to a well-known land-living hunter: wolves. Just as wolves hunt in packs, using teamwork to bring down large prey, orcas cooperate when hunting in groups called pods. Different pods use different hunting techniques and target different prey animals. Some pods will gather in a tight group, then charge toward a seal resting out of reach on an ice floe. This creates a wave that knocks the seal into the water, where they can grab it. Other pods blow air bubbles to herd schools of fish into a ball near the water's surface. The orcas then slap the ball with their tails, stunning the fish so they're easy to gobble down.

These sophisticated hunting techniques take a lot of brainpower. Orcas are considered among the most intelligent animals on Earth. They're even known to pass down their behaviors, such as hunting techniques, a taste for certain types of food, and unique vocalizations, from one generation to the next—one of only a few species on Earth known to do so.

Orca **PODS** in **NEIGHBORING WATERS** have different **VOCALIZATIONS**, like **HUMAN ACCENTS** that vary from one region to the next.

That's
Fact-tastic!

Like other dolphins, **ORCAS SLEEP** by **RESTING ONE HALF** of their **BRAIN** at a **TIME**. The **OTHER HALF STAYS AWAKE**. It **MONITORS** the surroundings for **PREDATORS** and **OBSTACLES** and also **SIGNALS** the animal **WHEN IT'S TIME TO RISE** to the **SURFACE** for a **BREATH** of **AIR**.

185

SEA SMARTS

Whales and dolphins can toss balls, jump through hoops, and perform all kinds of other tricks. In the wild, they use complex vocalizations to communicate and teamwork to hunt prey in clever ways. So just how smart are the mammals of the sea?

We already know that dolphins and whales are expert communicators (p. 174). Scientists hope that someday we'll even know what they're saying! Whales and dolphins sing, click, and chatter to converse with their family group and cooperate for hunting. But how else can we measure their intelligence?

One test that experts often use to judge intelligence is called the mirror test. They'll show an animal its reflection to see if it recognizes itself. Many human children don't begin to recognize themselves in a mirror until they are a few years old. But the mirror test reveals that dolphins have this skill at just seven months! Dolphins will spin and pose in front of a mirror to watch their movements. They'll even use the mirror to investigate parts of their own bodies they don't normally see, such as the inside of their mouths!

Experts agree that another strong sign of intelligence is the ability to use tools. Only a few animals on Earth are known to use tools, including humans and other great apes, crows—and dolphins. One group of bottlenose dolphins in Australia uses sea sponges for hunting. A pod member will grab a sponge in its mouth, then use it to poke at the seafloor, flushing out fish for snacking. The sponge protects the dolphin's nose from scrapes—just like we might use gloves to protect our hands when digging in the dirt. Other dolphins and whales use mud, bubbles, or waves to help them hunt. Groups will even pass these techniques from one generation to the next!

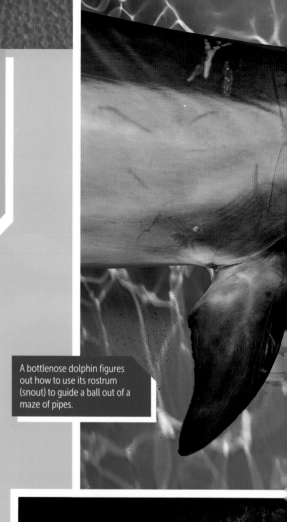

A bottlenose dolphin figures out how to use its rostrum (snout) to guide a ball out of a maze of pipes.

WHALES and **DOLPHINS** often use **TEAMWORK** to hunt.

Whales engage in "bubble-net feeding," a cooperative hunting method in which they dive beneath schools of fish, blow bubbles to stun them, and then surround the fish in an attempt to trap them.

MAMMAL MINDS

It's tough to measure the intelligence of any animal. Partly that's because they are so different from us. No other animals think or communicate exactly the same way humans do. Animals don't use complex math, build machines, or paint portraits. It's even harder to judge the smarts of ocean animals, because they are adapted to live in an environment totally different from ours. Even so, there are a few similarities between us and the mammals of the sea. Like humans, for example, many dolphins and whales are social animals. Also like humans, they have big brains for their body size. And finally, like humans and the great apes, their brains have special cells, called spindle neurons, used for advanced thinking, such as problem-solving and remembering. All these traits are clues that these seagoing creatures are mammal masterminds.

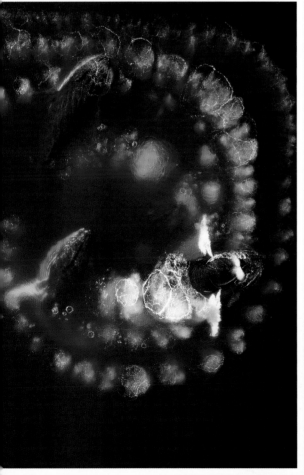

These bottlenose dolphins are working cooperatively to pull the cap off a container filled with fish.

CALIFORNIA SEA LION

FACTS

SCIENTIFIC NAME *Zalophus californianus*

GROUP NAME Colony, rookery

SIZE Up to 7.25 feet (2.2 m)

WEIGHT Up to 860 pounds (390 kg)

EATS Fish, squid, shellfish

A **GROUP** of **SEA LIONS FLOATING** in the water is called a **RAFT**.

Barking calls fill the air at a rocky outcrop on the California coastline. It's a colony of sea lions!

California sea lions gather by the hundreds. They honk, trumpet, roar, and bark. Baby sea lions bleat, calling to their mothers so each pair can find each other among all the other animals on the shore. A sea lion colony is one noisy place!

In the water, sea lions are sleek, agile swimmers. They can reach speeds of about 25 miles an hour (40 km/h) and stay beneath the surface for nearly 10 minutes at a time without having to come to the surface to breathe. Their swimming skills help them overtake their preferred prey of fish, squid, and shellfish. California sea lions can hunt without stopping for 30 hours at a time.

On land, sea lions aren't so graceful—though, unlike seals, sea lions can rotate their hind flippers forward to help them scoot along shorelines. They are most at home in the water, but they have to come on land to breed. In the spring, male sea lions, called bulls, will leave the ocean to claim a territory on ice, rocks, or a beach. They try to gather up as many females, called cows, as they can. Bulls spend weeks guarding this group, called a harem, and doing nothing else—not even eating!

Sea lion pups are usually born on land. Thirty minutes after birth, they are able to scoot around the shore. Sea lion mothers are attentive parents, nuzzling their pups and picking them up by the scruff of the neck. Mother sea lions alternate between nursing their babies and hunting for food. When they head for the water, their pups stay in a close group. When a mother sea lion gets back from a hunting trip, she and her pup call back and forth to find each other on the beach.

That's Fact-tastic!

SEALS and SEA LIONS look VERY SIMILAR. You can tell the DIFFERENCE by LOOKING at the ANIMAL'S EARS: While SEALS have only a TINY OPENING for their ears, SEA LIONS have SMALL FLAPS that cover theirs.

ELEPHANT SEALS were once hunted almost to **EXTINCTION** for their **BLUBBER,** which can be turned into oil. But now they are a **PROTECTED SPECIES,** and their **NUMBERS** have **REBOUNDED.**

ELEPHANT SEAL

It's no secret how this animal got its name: Male elephant seals have noses that look a bit like an elephant's trunk. Their noses are not only large in size—they're inflatable! During breeding season, male elephant seals blow up their noses and use them to produce a sound like a drum. This signals to other elephant seals in the area how big and strong they are and warns smaller, weaker males to stay away.

There are two species of elephant seals, the northern and the southern. Northern elephant seals live in the mild climate of California, U.S.A., and Baja California, Mexico, while southern elephant seals live in the extremely cold waters around Antarctica. Southern elephant seals are the largest seals on Earth. At up to 9,000 pounds (4,082 kg), they can weigh as much as a pickup truck! These massive animals have few predators to worry about: Killer whales and sharks are the only creatures that view them as prey.

Elephant seals spend nearly all their lives at sea, coming to shore only to molt (or shed their coat), mate, and give birth. While at sea, elephant seals spend much of their time diving deep below the surface to get to their favorite prey: bottom dwellers such as ratfish, eels, and rockfish.

When northern elephant seal pups are born, they grow quickly on a diet of mother's milk—which is 55 percent fat. (The whole cow's milk that humans drink is about 3.5 percent fat.) On this rich diet, a pup grows from about 75 pounds (34 kg) at birth to as much as 350 pounds (159 kg) in less than a month. Some clever pups nurse from several females. These big eaters can weigh 600 pounds (272 kg)!

FACTS

SCIENTIFIC NAME *Mirounga* (genus)

GROUP NAME Colony

SIZE Up to 20 feet (6.1 m)

WEIGHT Up to 4.5 tons (4.1 t)

EATS Bottom-dwelling fish

SOUTHERN ELEPHANT SEAL PUPS

Seals use their **SHORT FRONT FLIPPERS** to **FLOP ALONG** on their **BELLIES,** a way of **MOVING CALLED GALUMPHING.**

MANATEE

FACTS

SCIENTIFIC NAME *Trichechus* (genus)

GROUP NAME Herd

SIZE Up to 13 feet (4 m)

WEIGHT Up to 1,300 pounds (590 kg)

EATS Seagrass, mangrove leaves, algae

MANATEES are the **LARGEST PLANT-EATERS** in the **OCEAN.**

The manatee rests in shallow water, propped up on its tail with its head above the surface. This behavior, called "tail standing," may be the reason that explorers once mistook manatees for mermaids—even though these roly-poly animals look nothing like beautiful fish-tailed maidens!

There are three different species of manatee. The West Indian manatee roams along the east coast of Florida and all the way down to Brazil. The Amazonian manatee lives in South America's Amazon River. And the West African manatee swims along the west coast and rivers of Africa. Manatees need warm water to survive. Even though they look like they have blubber to keep them warm, a manatee's big, round body is mostly made up of its stomach and intestines, not fat. Because of this, manatees need water that is 60°F (16°C) or warmer. Sometimes, manatees that live in Florida will even gather near the discharge pipes of power plants, which pump heated water into the ocean. They love to relax in the warm water!

These animals are often called sea cows—and at up to 1,300 pounds (590 kg) they weigh nearly as much as a cow! Also like cows, they are grazers. Manatees feed on seagrass, mangrove leaves, and algae. It takes a lot of plant matter to fuel their big bodies, so manatees spend about half of every day eating. They can chow down on 150 pounds (68 kg) of food each day.

The manatee's gentle nature and habit of living along the coastline often puts it in close contact with humans. In the past, people would hunt these animals for their hides, oil, and bones. By the early 1990s, there were just about 1,300 West Indian manatees left off the coast of Florida. Today, manatees are protected by U.S. law, and their population in Florida numbers more than 6,000.

That's Fact-tastic!

DUGONGS are a COUSIN of the MANATEE. Although the two species look similar, DUGONGS have a tail, or FLUKE, that LOOKS LIKE a WHALE'S, while manatees have rounded flukes that look like paddles. And while some manatees live in freshwater, DUGONGS LIVE ONLY in the OCEAN.

MANATEE

POLAR BEAR

FACTS

SCIENTIFIC NAME *Ursus maritimus*

GROUP NAME Celebration

SIZE Up to 8 feet (2.4 m)

WEIGHT Up to 1,600 pounds (726 kg)

EATS Seals, whale carcasses

The adult male polar bear rears up on its hind legs, sniffing the air. Standing like this, he is a towering 10 feet (3 m) tall, the largest predator to walk the land today.

Bears of many species are good swimmers. But polar bears are totally dependent on the Arctic Ocean for their food and habitat. That makes them marine mammals—the only species of bear on Earth classified this way. Polar bears have huge, slightly webbed front paws, which they use to paddle through the water. Individuals have been spotted swimming hundreds of miles offshore. To stay warm in the frigid water, they have a lush coat of fur, black skin to help absorb heat, and a thick layer of insulating blubber.

When they aren't in the water, polar bears spend much of their time hunting. They usually eat seals, and they tend to hunt their prey around areas where the sea ice is shifting and cracking. Polar bears will stay motionless near the ice edge or a seal breathing hole, waiting for a seal to come to the surface. When it does, the bear will bite or grab the seal and pull it onto the ice. Polar bears have such a strong sense of smell that they can detect a seal beneath three feet (1 m) of snow.

Although they live in one of the coldest places on Earth, polar bears don't hibernate. Instead, they keep hunting right through the winter. The only polar bears that seek shelter during the cold of winter are pregnant females. They dig deep into snow drifts to create a sheltered area for their cubs. There, they give birth—almost always to twins!

The polar bear's **SCIENTIFIC NAME,** *Ursus maritimus,* means **"SEA BEAR."**

That's
Fact-tastic!

POLAR BEAR FUR is
NOT WHITE. It's actually
TRANSLUCENT, or see-through.
Polar bears look white because of
the way the AIR SPACES in the
HAIRS SCATTER LIGHT and
REFLECT it back to OUR EYES.
This white appearance
helps CAMOUFLAGE polar
bears in their SNOW-
COVERED HOME.

EXTINCT MARINE MAMMALS

Polar bears and blue whales certainly are impressive animals. But some of the most remarkable marine mammals ever to swim in Earth's oceans are creatures of the past. From a manatee relative the size of a bus to a meat-eating mega-whale, meet some of the extinct ocean-dwelling mammals.

STELLER'S SEA COW

As recently as the mid-1700s, some sailors in the North Pacific Ocean spotted an extraordinary animal: a manatee relative longer than a bus. This supersize swimmer was a Steller's sea cow, and it was three times longer than a modern manatee. Before the last ice age began, about 2.6 million years ago, Steller's sea cows once lived everywhere from Japan to the Baja Peninsula, and they inhabited the chilly waters of the Arctic until as recently as about 250 years ago.

BASILOSAURUS

When its fossils were first discovered, this ancient creature was nicknamed "king lizard." But this animal was no reptile: It was a whale, and also the largest meat-eater of its time. Thirty-five million years ago, it stalked oceans around the world for prey. Scientists think this because they have discovered fossils of baby whales from a different, smaller species with bite marks from a *Basilosaurus* on their heads.

LIVYATAN MELVILLEI

Author Herman Melville wrote of a terrifying white whale powerful enough to sink a boat in his novel *Moby-Dick*. That creature was fictional, but in 2010, scientists in Peru reported the discovery of the fossil of a whale so fearsome that they named it *Livyatan melvillei* in Melville's honor. This 12-million-year-old sea mammal was about half as long as a basketball court and had jaws lined with foot-long (30-cm) teeth. Unlike the modern mega-whale, the blue whale, *Livyatan melvillei* hunted down prey and used these deadly teeth to eat it.

RODHOCETUS KASRANI

Forty-five million years ago in what is now Pakistan, an animal the size of a bear waddled along the shore. Then, spotting a potential meal in the water, it dived, using large webbed hooves to paddle into the sea. *Rodhocetus kasrani* had traits of both the land-dwelling ancestors of modern whales and of the ocean-living true whales that would come after it.

KOLPONOMOS

To open clams and mussels, modern sea otters (p. 176) bash the shells against rocks. A mysterious, extinct marine mammal named *Kolponomos* also ate shellfish—but it used its mouth to crack them open, a bit like a living bottle opener. Its crushing jaws exerted an enormous amount of force, giving it a bite similar to that of a saber-toothed cat. *Kolponomos* was a relative of modern bears, but it resembled no creature alive today.

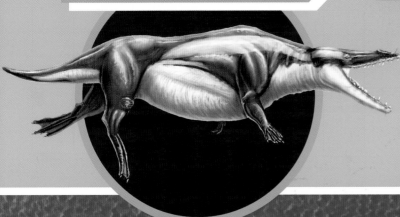

BLACK-AND-WHITE
RUFFED LEMUR

CHAPTER **SEVEN**

MONKEYS AND MORE

PRIMATES

ALL ABOUT PRIMATES

They swing through trees like furry acrobats. Some use their extra-long arms and tails—many designed for gripping, like an extra hand—primates leap, climb, and hang in forests around the world.

The primates are divided into three groups: the monkeys, the apes (which includes chimpanzees, gorillas, and orangutans), and the prosimians (which includes lemurs, lorises, and tarsiers). Most primates have forward-facing eyes, which help them judge distance, and keen vision. Most also have opposable thumbs, or thumbs that can bend to touch their other fingers, giving them a strong grip. These adaptations help them live life high in the treetops.

All primates have large brains compared to their body size. And many are known for their intelligence. Like dolphins and many other smart creatures, primates live in groups with others of their species. When they're not sleeping, they spend most of the time socializing as they forage for fruits, leaves, and nuts in the tropical forests where the majority of primates are found. Some primates also live in towns and cities. That's because humans are primates, too!

SOUTH AFRICAN GALAGO

SCIENTIFIC NAME: *Galago moholi*

SIZE: About 6.5 inches (17 cm) with a tail 4.5 to 11 inches (11–28 cm) long

WEIGHT: Up to 9 ounces (250 g)

EATS: Butterflies, moths, beetles, sap, plants

PYGMY MARMOSET

SCIENTIFIC NAME: *Callithrix pygmaea*

SIZE: About 5 inches (13 cm) with an 8-inch (20-cm) tail

WEIGHT: About 4.5 ounces (130 g)

EATS: Gum, sap, and resin from trees; also fruit and insects

MANDRILL

SCIENTIFIC NAME: *Mandrillus sphinx*

SIZE: Up to 30 inches (76 cm)

WEIGHT: Up to 120 pounds (54 kg)

EATS: Fruits, seeds, insects, snails, worms, frogs

AZARA'S NIGHT MONKEY

SCIENTIFIC NAME: *Aotus azarae*

SIZE: Up to 15 inches (38 cm)

WEIGHT: About 2 pounds (1 kg)

EATS: Insects, fruits, leaves, flowers, bird eggs, small vertebrates

GOLDEN SNUB-NOSED MONKEY

SCIENTIFIC NAME: *Rhinopithecus roxellana*

SIZE: Up to 30 inches (76 cm) with a tail about as long as its body

WEIGHT: Up to 40 pounds (18 kg)

EATS: Leaves, bark, grains, nuts, lichens

Just because orangutans **LIVE OUTSIDE** where they are exposed to the elements **DOESN'T** mean they **LIKE** to get **WET.** When it **RAINS,** orangutans often **GRAB LARGE LEAVES** and hold them **OVERHEAD** to **SHELTER** themselves from the falling drops—the same way **HUMANS** use **UMBRELLAS!**

ORANGUTAN

High up in the trees, an orange-furred animal uses its long arms to swing from branch to branch. This acrobat of the rainforest is an orangutan. It spends nearly its entire life in the treetops, even making nests in the branches for sleeping.

When orangutans stand, their fingers nearly touch the ground. They have such long arms that if a full-grown male orangutan stretches them out, they can span seven feet (2.1 m) from fingertip to fingertip. They also have feet that work just like hands. Together, these adaptations help them move through the trees with ease. Even baby orangutans can scamper through the treetops. If they come upon a gap between branches that's too wide to cross, their mother will use her body to make a bridge so the baby can climb across.

There are three species of orangutans. The Bornean orang-utan lives on the island of Borneo. The Sumatran orangutan and Tapanuli orangutan live on the island of Sumatra. Both islands, which are in Southeast Asia, have rainforests that hold many fruit-bearing trees. Orangutans' favorite food is fruit. They eat more than 300 species, including figs and durians, spine-covered fruits with a strong smell. They also eat nuts, bark, and occasionally insects such as ants and termites. When they get thirsty, they sip water from holes in trees or lick it off leaves.

Male orangutans prefer to spend most of their time alone, but female orangutans and their offspring form close bonds. Infants will stay with their mothers until they learn survival skills such as how to build a treetop nest and where to find ripe fruit at different times of the year. There's so much to learn about life in the rainforest that this can take eight or nine years!

FACTS

SCIENTIFIC NAME *Pongo* (genus)

GROUP NAME None

SIZE Up to 5 feet (1.5 m)

WEIGHT Up to 180 pounds (81 kg)

EATS Mostly fruit

Orangutans are the LARGEST ANIMALS on EARTH that EAT PRIMARILY FRUIT— though they also EAT OTHER FOODS such as leaves and nuts.

CHIMPANZEES, BONOBOS, AND YOU

DNA makes you who you are; it's the genetic material that's passed down from generation to generation. And more than 98 percent of human DNA is identical to the DNA of two other animals on the planet: the chimpanzee and the bonobo. These creatures are our closest living cousins. In fact, chimpanzees and bonobos are more closely related to humans than they are to gorillas!

Humans, chimpanzees, and bonobos all shared an ancestor that lived in Africa between six and eight million years ago. Because it is rare for bones to become fossils in the hot, wet environment of the rainforest, experts have not yet discovered fossils of this ape ancestor, so what it looked like and even where it lived are still a mystery. But in 2014, scientists made a major discovery when they unearthed the skull of a 13-million-year-old infant ape in Kenya, nicknamed "Alesi." Alesi was a fruit-eating primate that climbed slowly through the trees

BONOBO

BONOBOS

CHIMPANZEES and BONOBOS can RECOGNIZE themselves in a MIRROR, something that very few animals can do.

with long arms. Scientists think Alesi may reveal what the most recent ancestor of all living apes, including humans, looked like.

Chimpanzees, bonobos, and humans may look different on the outside, but we have the same bones, muscles, and nervous systems. Though a human's brain is larger than the brains of our closest cousins, it has the exact same structure. That suggests that chimpanzees and bonobos probably think very similarly to the way humans do. Their senses of sight, smell, hearing, and touch are nearly identical to ours, too.

Chimpanzees, humans, and bonobos have other similarities, too. Recent studies show that, like humans, bonobos are kind to strangers, sharing food even when they don't get any themselves. Other studies show that we all may share an understanding of basic body language. Chimpanzees and bonobos often ask another troop member to groom them by scratching a shoulder. They may fling a hand out sideways to tell a companion to move away. Humans have no trouble understanding these signals. And all three species wave their hands to greet each other—and even laugh when they are tickled!

CHIMPANZEES are known to **KISS** each other.

CHIMPANZEES

GORILLA

FACTS

SCIENTIFIC NAME *Gorilla* (genus)

GROUP NAME Troop

SIZE Up to 6 feet (1.8 m)

WEIGHT 400 pounds (181 kg)

EATS Leaves, stems, fruit, seeds, roots, ants, termites

Each gorilla has **UNIQUE FINGERPRINTS** and also **UNIQUE NOSE PRINTS.**

When the leader of a gorilla troop feels threatened, he may stand upright, throw nearby sticks and rocks, pound his huge chest with both fists, and let out a deafening roar. But it's all for show. Though they may look intimidating, gorillas are generally peaceful animals that live in complex social groups.

There are two groups of gorillas: mountain gorillas, which inhabit the green, volcanic mountains of Central Africa; and lowland gorillas, which live in the flat forests of Central and West Africa. Gorillas are the largest of all primates. Too big to swing through the trees like their cousins, they spend most of their time on the ground, foraging for plants. An adult male gorilla can eat 40 pounds (18 kg) of food each day, using strong jaws and teeth to chew through tough stems.

A group of gorillas is called a troop. A gorilla troop usually has between five and 30 individuals, led by a strong, mature male called a silverback because of the gray hairs that grow on his back. The silverback decides when his troop will travel, when it will rest, and where it will spend the night. Each morning, he leads the troop to a new area to eat. After their morning meal, each adult gorilla builds a nest out of leaves, twigs, and branches, then takes a nap. After they wake up from their snooze, the gorillas eat again until bedtime, when they make another nest to spend the night in.

Gorillas are humans' closest cousins after chimpanzees and bonobos. And they have many humanlike behaviors and emotions, such as laughter and sadness. They use complex signals to communicate with each other. They may crouch down low when being submissive or stand tall when confident. Scientists have recorded them using 22 different vocalizations, including screams, barks, and roars.

That's
Fact-tastic!

Mother gorillas carry their **BABIES** against their **CHESTS** for their **FIRST** few **MONTHS** of life. When the **BABY** is **OLD** enough, it **CLINGS** to Mom's **BACK** so she can use her hands to **FORAGE** for food. **BABY GORILLAS STAY** with their **MOTHERS** until they are about **FOUR YEARS OLD.**

AMAZING APES

GORILLAS

Stare into a chimpanzee's eyes and you might get the feeling that it is staring back at you with the same curiosity. The great apes—chimpanzees, bonobos, orangutans, and gorillas—share their family group with humans. They have humanlike hands and faces, as well as humanlike habits, such as cradling their babies against their chests. So just how humanlike are their brains?

In the 1960s, ape expert Jane Goodall made a discovery that shocked the world: She saw chimpanzees in what is now Gombe, Tanzania, using twigs to "fish" for termites by poking them into termite mounds. The chimps would pick a leafy twig and then strip off the leaves to make the perfect termite-grabbing tool. It was the first time anyone had observed an animal other than humans making and using tools. Now scientists know that chimps are animal tool

JANE GOODALL
WITH CHIMPANZEES

SECOND SMARTEST?

Chimpanzees and gorillas may be intelligent, but humans are still the world's smartest creature ... right? In 2007, for the first time, chimpanzees outperformed humans in a task designed to test their smarts. Three adult female chimps and their three five-year-old offspring went head-to-head with university student volunteers in a memory game that tasked them with memorizing the location of numbers as they appeared in random spots around a screen. The adult chimps performed about the same as the humans at the task. But amazingly, the young chimps did even better!

ALLTALK-4

ALLTALK-

Kanzi gets a hug from researcher Sue Savage-Rumbaugh after successfully completing a quiz.

KANZI

masters, using objects such as leaves and rocks to clean themselves, gather food, and defend their territories. They even pass on what they've learned from one generation to the next, which makes scientists consider their behavior a type of culture.

Humans are the only animals known to use language to communicate. But that might not be because we have superior brains—it might simply be because we have the ability to speak. A lowland gorilla named Koko, who lived from 1971 to 2018, learned to use more than a thousand signs in American Sign Language and could understand about 2,000 words of spoken English. She showed her human teachers that apes can have a sense of humor and feel grief—even whimpering in sadness when her pet kitten died.

Later, experts taught a chimpanzee named Kanzi to communicate using a keyboard of symbols. Kanzi learned more than 3,000 spoken English words and could convey his own ideas using his keyboard, such as typing the symbols for "marshmallow" and "fire." When researchers gave him marshmallows and matches, he snapped twigs, built a fire, lit it, and toasted his sweets on a stick.

One group of chimpanzees in Senegal, West Africa, makes SPEARS OUT OF STICKS, then uses them to hunt primates called galagos.

GIBBON

FACTS

SCIENTIFIC NAME Hylobatidae (family)

GROUP NAME Family

SIZE Up to 25 inches (64 cm)

WEIGHT Up to 29 pounds (13 kg)

EATS Mostly fruit

RED-CHEEKED GIBBON

When gibbons WALK along TREE BRANCHES, they hold their ARMS OUT for BALANCE, like tightrope walkers.

A gibbon swings through the rainforest. Using its extraordinarily long arms and hook-shaped hands, it moves from branch to branch at up to 35 miles an hour (56 km/h), about as fast as a galloping racehorse! Using this unique way of moving, called brachiating, it can fling itself across gaps between the trees as wide as 50 feet (15 m).

While most primates change partners throughout their lives, gibbons are monogamous: They form long-term bonds and sometimes mate for life. A gibbon pair lives with its young in a group called a family. They choose a territory in the South Asian rainforest where they live, then warn other gibbon families to keep out by singing out in loud, complex songs. Entire gibbon families will sing together, sometimes using specially adapted throat pouches that make their calls louder. Gibbon families begin each day by singing at sunrise.

Gibbons spend most of their time in the treetops, snacking on fruit or moving through the forest to find their next meal. But they do occasionally come down to the ground, and when they do, they walk on two feet, holding their long arms above their heads to help them balance. They are more comfortable walking on two feet than any other primate, aside from humans. Scientists study gibbon locomotion to find clues for how human ancestors may have begun walking millions of years ago.

Gibbons are often confused with monkeys, but they are not monkeys. Instead, they are part of the ape family, sometimes called the "lesser apes" because they are smaller in size than the great apes, which include gorillas, chimpanzees, and humans. There are more than a dozen species of gibbon known so far. The most recently described species, announced in 2017, is called the Skywalker hoolock gibbon, named for the character Luke Skywalker from *Star Wars*.

That's Fact-tastic!

The **LARGEST SPECIES** of gibbon is the **SIAMANG.** If it **STRETCHES** its **ARMS OUT,** they can **SPAN** nearly **FIVE FEET** (1.5 m)— about as long as a **HOCKEY STICK!**

WHITE-HANDED GIBBON

That's
Fact-tastic!

The **WHITE CREST** on the cotton-top tamarin's **HEAD** isn't just for looks. When **THREATENED,** the monkeys **RAISE** this **FUR** up. That makes these monkeys **APPEAR LARGER** than they really are, helping them **SCARE** off **PREDATORS** or intimidate **RIVALS.**

COTTON-TOP TAMARIN

It's no mystery how these monkeys got their name: They have a thick tuft of white hair on their heads! At just about the size of a squirrel, cotton-top tamarins are one of the smallest primates on Earth.

Cotton-top tamarins live only in one small forest in north-western Colombia. There, they hop and climb through the trees, on the hunt for fruits and insects to snack on. These primates are known for their unique clawlike nails, which help them cling to the tree bark as they leap from branch to branch. Their small home range puts cotton-top tamarins in jeopardy: Colombia is losing much of its tamarin habitat as humans cut down trees to make way for farms and houses.

These monkeys depend on the rainforest for survival, but the rainforest depends on them, too. Cotton-top tamarins help keep the forest healthy by eating fruits that other primates don't, then spreading those seeds to new locations in their droppings. Tamarin poop even makes great fertilizer for new plants to sprout. That makes these monkeys rainforest farmers!

For tamarins, parenthood is a big job. Tamarin babies are big—about a quarter of the size of a full-grown adult—and they are almost always born as twins. These monkeys live in close family groups, and all adults help take care of the babies, even carrying them on their backs to give moms a break. The tamarins also work together to fend off predators like snakes and large cats. These monkeys may be small, but teamwork makes them tough!

FACTS

SCIENTIFIC NAME *Saguinus oedipus*

GROUP NAME Troop

SIZE Up to 10 inches (25 cm) with a tail up to 16 inches (40 cm) long

WEIGHT Up to 20 ounces (567 g)

EATS Fruit, insects

Each cotton-top tamarin **FAVORS** its own **INSECT-HUNTING TECHNIQUES,** such as sneaking up, turning over leaves, and checking nearby crevices.

TARSIER

FACTS

SCIENTIFIC NAME Tarsiidae (family)

GROUP NAME Troop

SIZE Up to 6 inches (16 cm) with a tail up to 12 inches (32 cm) long

WEIGHT About 5 ounces (142 g)

EATS Insects, small reptiles

This tiny, big-eyed primate looks too adorable to exist. But the tarsier (TAR-see-ur) is a real-life animal the size of a stick of butter that bounces through the forests of Indonesia, the Philippines, and the island of Borneo.

The tarsier's most striking feature is its enormous eyes. They are the biggest eyes relative to body size of any mammal on Earth. In fact, they're so big that the tarsier can't rotate them. Instead, it looks around by swiveling its head almost 360 degrees, like an owl. To process all the information coming in from those oversize eyes, the tarsier's brain has a huge section devoted to vision.

Those big eyes evolved to give the tarsier extraordinary night vision. Tarsiers snooze during the day and hunt at night. They are the only completely carnivorous primates, eating only insects, lizards, and snakes. They cling upright to trees with their long, padded fingers, pressing their tail against the trunk for extra support. When they spot a tasty meal, they launch themselves from the trunk to snag their snack. Tarsiers can hop from tree to tree so quickly their bodies look like a blur!

Scientists studying these tiny acrobats noticed that tarsiers often stare around them with their mouths open—yet make no sound. At least, no sound that humans can hear. In fact, they are using echolocation, like a bat, chirping away at superhigh frequencies that our ears can't detect. They are among the only primates to do so. Experts aren't sure why they do it, but one theory is that they use their ultrasonic sounds to call to other tarsiers without other animals overhearing, like a secret language.

Even though **THEY'RE TINY, TARSIERS** can **LEAP** up to **16 FEET** (5 m).

That's **Fact-tastic!**

Tarsiers have **EXTRA-LONG FINGERS** with **STICKY PADS** on each **FINGERTIP.** These unusual digits give tarsiers **EXTRA GRIP** so that they can **LEAP** from **TREE** to **TREE WITH EASE,** helping make them **EXPERT CLIMBERS.** The second and third toes of their hind feet are tipped in claws, which tarsiers use to **GROOM** themselves.

215

SOCIAL LIFE

Mother orangutans and their young enjoy a snack of sunflower seeds.

They sunbathe with their friends, comb through each other's hair, and even hug. But this doesn't just describe the activities of humans: These are the behaviors of a number of primates! Many primates—including humans—live in social groups that often include members of their families. This way of life shapes their behavior.

Group living has advantages. Buddying up with a group helps protect primates from predators: With multiple eyes watching for danger and large numbers to defend against attackers, it's often safer than attempting to survive alone. Large numbers of individuals are also better at finding food. That's especially useful for many primates. They must remember which trees in their large territories have ripe fruit, and during what time of year.

Humans use language to communicate with our groupmates. Other primates communicate, too, but they use body language and vocalizations. Howler monkeys' (p. 220) booming calls warn competing troops to keep out of their way. Lemurs (p. 222) call to each other in quiet voices to keep the group together as they forage. Male baboons open their mouths wide in warning. And gorillas (p. 206) beat their chests to scare away rivals.

BONOBOS

BONOBO and LEMUR groups are both LED by FEMALES. Other mammals with FEMALE LEADERS are orcas, lions, elephants, and spotted hyenas.

Primate groups are usually organized in hierarchies, with the most important, dominant animal as the leader. Being higher up in the hierarchy means more access to food and mates. The hierarchy is constantly changing, meaning that animals in a group have to keep track of many shifting social relationships at the same time. Some experts think this is why many of Earth's most intelligent animals are social. Many primates use grooming to keep their place in the hierarchy. Chimpanzees groom each other to keep the peace after disagreements, and one chimp is more likely to share food with another chimp that has groomed it. Humans don't pick parasites off each other, but we do give high fives, hugs, and pats on the shoulder—all touches that show our social bonds.

A pair of rhesus macaques groom each other.

RING-TAILED LEMUR

LIVING SOLO

While most primates are social, the prosimians—the group that includes tarsiers and lorises—are solitary animals. They are mostly nocturnal, shy creatures that hide in the treetops to stay safe from predators. Other than when females are caring for their young, they mostly keep to themselves. Of all the apes, orangutans are the only ones that are mostly solitary.

BABOON

SPIDER MONKEY

FACTS

SCIENTIFIC NAME *Ateles* (genus)

GROUP NAME Troop

SIZE Up to 26 inches (66 cm)

WEIGHT About 13 pounds (6 kg)

EATS Insects, fruit

Spider monkeys use their long, grasping tail like a fifth limb. The tail grabs on to branches, giving the monkey a boost as it moves through the forest. Sometimes, spider monkeys even hang upside down from their tails with their arms and legs dangling. When they do that, they look a bit like spiders—that's how they got their name!

Spider monkeys live in the rainforests of Central and South America and as far north as Mexico. They are perfectly adapted to life high in the trees, with long limbs and flexible shoulder joints that allow them to swing easily from branch to branch. They also have hooklike hands great for grasping branches. Even the spider monkey's tail is well suited for treetop living, with a pad on its end much like the palm of a hand that gives the monkey extra clinging power.

These primates are highly social, gathering during the day in groups that can number more than three dozen. They spend the daylight hours foraging for food and will eat just about anything they find in the forest, including nuts, fruits, leaves, and bird eggs. When spider monkeys are around, the forest rings with their many calls and screeches. At night, spider monkeys split off into smaller groups and cuddle up together. These monkeys are so at home in the trees that they even sleep there!

Like human infants, spider monkey babies need constant care. Monkey mothers carry their babies on their bellies for the first four months of life, then switch to carrying them piggyback-style. Young spider monkeys aren't ready to leave their mothers and fend for themselves until they are about a year old.

Spider monkeys are known to **HUG EACH OTHER.** When they do, they sometimes **WRAP** their **TAILS** around **EACH OTHER'S BODIES.**

That's **Fact-tastic!**

Unlike just about every other primate, **SPIDER MONKEYS DON'T** have **THUMBS.** Experts say that's because the digit could snag on tree limbs. Instead, spider monkeys' **HANDS FORM** a **HOOK** perfect for **GRABBING BRANCHES** as they swing through the forest.

Howler monkeys almost **NEVER COME** down to the **GROUND.** One of the few times they **VENTURE OUT** of the trees is during times of **DROUGHT** when they need to **FIND WATER.** Most of the time, they can get almost all the **WATER** they need from the **FOOD THEY EAT.**

HOWLER MONKEY

As the rising sun makes the rainforest begin to glow with dim light, a spooky sound fills the air. It sounds like the cries of a terrible monster. But it's actually just a troop of howler monkeys greeting the dawn.

Howler monkeys' name is no exaggeration: In fact, these South American primates are the loudest land animal in the Western Hemisphere! Male monkeys have a cavity in one of their throat bones. When they pull air through this hole, it makes their calls extra loud. Under the right conditions, a howler monkey's call can be heard from about three miles (4.8 km) away! Howlers typically call at dawn and dusk. Their cries are a message to other monkeys saying "Keep away! This territory is ours!"

There are several species of howler monkey that live in Central and South America. They are the largest monkeys in the Americas, reaching up to three feet (1 m) long, with a tail as long as their body. Like many other monkeys, they use this prehensile, or grasping, tail as an extra limb to help them move through the forest. Howlers usually sit in the highest branches, feeding mostly on leaves. Because leaves are plentiful in the rainforest, howlers don't have to travel far to find food. They typically only move the length of a few football fields in a day.

Howler troops are usually led by an older male monkey. In one species, the black howler monkey, males are about twice as heavy as females. The males also have a black coat, while females are blonde. They are one of the few primates that have males and females of different colors.

FACTS

SCIENTIFIC NAME *Alouatta* (genus)

GROUP NAME Troop

SIZE Up to 3 feet (1 m) with a tail up to 3 feet (1 m) long

WEIGHT Up to 22 pounds (10 kg)

EATS Mostly leaves, also flowers and fruits

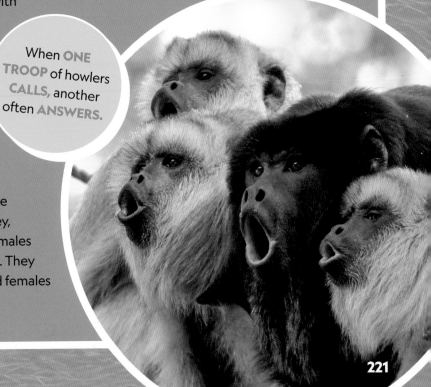

When **ONE TROOP** of howlers **CALLS,** another often **ANSWERS.**

MEET THE
LEMURS

Lemurs live in only one place in the world: the island of Madagascar, 250 miles (402 km) off the east coast of Africa. Lemurs are the world's oldest living primates. Their ancestors roamed Africa side by side with the dinosaurs, more than 70 million years ago. Scientists think they floated their way to Madagascar on "rafts" of matted vegetation. Today, lemurs are considered among the most endangered groups of mammals on the planet.

SIFAKA

Sifakas have an unusual way of moving: They stay upright, like small humans, leaping through the trees by springing on their hind legs. They can jump more than 20 feet (6.1 m) this way! On the ground, these lemurs don't move on all fours like other lemurs. Instead, they hop sideways on their hind legs. This makes them look a bit like they are dancing!

RING-TAILED LEMUR

When the sun is out, ring-tailed lemurs like to catch some rays, sitting with their bellies pointed toward the sun and their arms and legs stretched out. When they're nice and warm, the lemurs forage for leaves, flowers, and insects. Ring-tailed lemurs live in social groups, called troops, of up to 30 individuals. A dominant female is in charge. One glance from her and even her mate will give up his nice sunny napping spot or drop a piece of food so that she can have it.

BLUE-EYED BLACK LEMUR

This lemur is one of the only primates in the world with blue eyes. And that's not the only unusual thing about it. Blue-eyed black lemur males look totally different from the females. At first glance, they don't even seem to belong to the same species! Whereas the males are completely black, the females vary in shade from reddish brown to gray. Little is known about the habits of these animals, because they are some of the most endangered of all primates: There are only about 1,000 of these animals left in the wild.

MADAME BERTHE'S MOUSE LEMUR

Small enough to fit in a teacup, this is the smallest lemur and the world's smallest primate. At up to 1.2 ounces (34 g), they weigh only about as much as a pencil. They have huge eyes equipped with a reflective membrane, like a cat's, that allows them to see very well at night. That's when these miniature lemurs emerge to search for fruits, flowers, and insects. During the colder months, they are able to enter a state called torpor, like bears (p. 34) do, in which their hearts and other body systems slow down.

AYE-AYE

This is one odd animal. The aye-aye uses its extra-long, skinny middle finger to *tap-tap-tap* on a tree trunk. Its radar-like ears listen intently for insect larvae wriggling under the bark. When it hears a tasty snack, the aye-aye bores a hole in the tree with its sharp teeth—which never stop growing, like a rodent's. Then it digs out the larvae with that long middle finger. Yum!

PYGMY SLOW LORIS

FACTS

SCIENTIFIC NAME *Nycticebus pygmaeus*

GROUP NAME None

SIZE Up to 10 inches (25 cm)

WEIGHT Around 1 pound (0.5 kg)

EATS Fruit, tree sap, insects

A pygmy slow loris hangs upside down by its feet, using both plump hands to eat a piece of fruit. As it munches, it watches the dark forest with its enormous round eyes. Slow lorises are among the rarest and most endangered primates on Earth. They are also the only primate species with a venomous bite.

Because there are so few of them, and they are only active at night, little is known about the pygmy slow loris. This unusual animal's most noticeable trait is its huge eyes. Packed with light receptors, they help it navigate the trees to search for food at night. Pygmy slow lorises live in the rainforests and evergreen forests of southern China, eastern Cambodia, Laos, and Vietnam. They are the smallest of the slow loris species, weighing about as much as a football.

When slow lorises lick glands on their upper arms, their saliva mixes with a secretion to become venom. Slow lorises don't have many defenses such as claws or powerful jaws. But with its deadly bite, the slow loris can defend itself from predators such as pythons and eagles. Mother slow lorises will even lick their young, covering them in venom, before leaving them to find food. That spiked spit tells predators "Keep away from my baby!"

With their furry faces and big round eyes, slow lorises are incredibly adorable. Unfortunately, this cuteness has put them in danger. Poachers shine bright lights into the trees, disorienting the lorises, which they then grab and sell as pets. But these forest dwellers are sensitive animals that don't usually survive in captivity. Now several organizations aim to educate people about slow lorises in the pet trade, in the hopes of keeping these endearing creatures where they belong: in the forest.

Like the Madame Berthe's mouse lemur, the pygmy slow loris also goes into **TORPOR**, a **HIBERNATION-LIKE STATE**, in the winter. They are two of only a few species of primates that do this.

That's
Fact-tastic!

During the winter, when fruit is scarce, slow lorises switch to **EATING TREE SAP.** They have **SHARP TEETH** that they use to **DRILL INTO** the **BARK** of a tree, causing sap to flow from the hole. Then the lorises lick up the sap.

EXTINCT PRIMATES

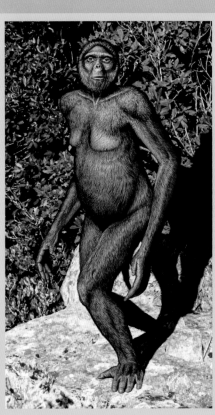

Primates have been climbing around in Earth's forests for more than 50 million years. The earliest primates were rat-size animals, but their descendants would adapt and evolve to become expert tree dwellers. Fast-forward a few more million years and one group of primates would come down to the forest floor for the first time. They were the ancestors of *Homo sapiens* (us).

ARCHICEBUS ACHILLES

Some 55 million years ago, a tiny primate scurried through the trees of what is now central China. It was *Archicebus achilles*, the earliest primate yet discovered. When it was alive, most of the planet was covered in tropical forests—there were even palm trees in what is now Alaska! *Archicebus achilles* was about the size of a human hand and weighed less than an ounce (28 g), making it smaller than the modern pygmy mouse lemur. Experts say it may show that primates likely originated in Asia.

"ARDI"

Around 4.4 million years ago, an ancient primate swung through the trees like an ape—but could perhaps also come down to the forest floor and walk on two legs like a human. This was *Ardipithecus ramidus*, nicknamed Ardi. This primate was about the height and weight of a modern chimpanzee. Ardi lived at an important period in history, shortly after our ancestors split off from the ancestors of chimpanzees. Experts think Ardi may be the earliest human ancestor to walk on two legs ever discovered.

GIGANTOPITHECUS

Imagine an ape that was as big as a polar bear. That was *Gigantopithecus blacki*, the biggest primate that ever lived. An extinct relative of the orangutan, it stood about 10 feet (3 m) tall and weighed up to 660 pounds (300 kg). This enormous ape roamed Southeast Asia for at least a million years and only went extinct around 100,000 years ago. That means it lived side by side with some species of early humans.

NEANDERTHAL

They are the closest extinct relatives of humans. Neanderthals (nee-AN-der-TALs) went extinct just 40,000 years ago, meaning they walked the planet at the same time as *Homo sapiens*—us. Experts have found thousands of Neanderthal fossils and artifacts, and they know more about these human cousins than about any other extinct human species. Neanderthals were short and stocky, with large noses and ridges on their foreheads. They made tools and jewelry, cared for sick companions, and even buried their dead.

"LUCY"

In 1974, scientists in the Afar desert of Ethiopia made an incredible discovery: the fossil remains of an early human ancestor. Forty percent of the skeleton had survived for 3.2 million years to the modern day, making the fossil, nicknamed Lucy, the most complete specimen of an early human ancestor that had ever been found at that time. Members of Lucy's genus, *Australopithecus*, existed right before our own genus, *Homo*, evolved. Like apes, they had small brains, but like humans, they walked on two legs.

CHAPTER **EIGHT**

MAMMAL ODDITIES

ALL ABOUT EARTH'S
STRANGEST MAMMALS

There are mammals that fly. There are mammals with spines instead of fur. And there are mammals totally unlike any other creature living today. Some are so puzzling that experts have spent centuries debating where to put them on the mammal family tree!

Some mammals in this chapter are unique because they have no living relatives. Platypuses (p. 232) and echidnas (p. 234) are mammals—but they lay eggs like birds or reptiles. They form their own ancient group of mammals, known as the monotremes. Then there are rabbits and hares. They may look similar to rodents, but along with pikas, they make up their own unique group.

Other mammals just do things differently from others in their family group. Giant pandas, for example, are members of the order Carnivora, with a digestive system designed to break down meat. But these bears are mostly vegetarians!

From a mouse with spines to an animal that smells like popcorn, these rule-breaking critters show the incredible variety of mammals that leap, climb, and scurry on planet Earth.

LONG-EARED JERBOA

SCIENTIFIC NAME: *Euchoreutes naso*

SIZE: About 3 inches (8 cm) with a 6-inch (15-cm) tail

WEIGHT: About 1 ounce (28 g)

EATS: Insects

STREAKED TENREC

SCIENTIFIC NAME: *Hemicentetes semispinosus*

SIZE: About 5.5 inches (14 cm)

WEIGHT: About 4.5 to 10 ounces (128–284 g)

EATS: Mostly worms

OKAPI

SCIENTIFIC NAME: *Okapia johnstoni*

SIZE: Up to 8.2 feet (2.5 m)

WEIGHT: Up to 770 pounds (350 kg)

EATS: Plants, sometimes dung

RACCOON DOG

SCIENTIFIC NAME: *Nyctereutes procyonoides*

SIZE: Up to 27 inches (70 cm)

WEIGHT: Up to 22 pounds (10 kg)

EATS: Fish, snakes, insects, small rodents, amphibians, birds, eggs

BRAZILIAN TAPIR

SCIENTIFIC NAME: *Tapirus terrestris*

SIZE: Up to 7.3 feet (2.2 m)

WEIGHT: Up to 550 pounds (250 kg)

EATS: Fruits, plants, seeds, grains, nuts

PLATYPUS

A mother platypus will hold the **EGGS BETWEEN** her **BODY** and her **TAIL** to keep them **WARM** until they **HATCH.**

The platypus looks like a mash-up of other animals: It has a bill and webbed feet like a duck's, a tail like a beaver's, and fur that looks like an otter's. On top of that, it's venomous! In fact, the first scientists to examine a platypus thought that someone was playing a joke on them.

So what is a platypus? It's a monotreme, or egg-laying mammal. There are only two kinds of monotremes on Earth; the others are the echidnas (p. 234). Along with the marsupials and placental mammals, the monotremes are one of the three main lineages of mammal alive today.

Monotremes live only in Australia and New Guinea. Like birds or reptiles, they lay eggs. But monotremes still have the characteristics that define mammals, such as fur. Monotremes even nurse their young with milk: After the eggs hatch, the babies lick milk that seeps from patches on the mother's belly.

The platypus's bill is bendy and feels like smooth leather. It's equipped with thousands of special sensors that can detect touch, pressure, sound waves, motion, and the slightest electrical currents. Platypuses are bottom-feeders that search river and stream bottoms for prey such as shellfish and insects, moving their bill back and forth. When they detect a tasty meal, they scoop it up, along with bits of gravel. Platypuses don't have teeth, so they use this gravel to grind up their food.

Platypuses dig burrows alongside rivers and streams, or shelter under rock ledges or tree roots. When they are ready to lay their eggs, female platypuses dig a deeper, more complex burrow with multiple chambers and entrances. When a mother platypus leaves her babies to go hunt for food, she plugs the entrance to the burrow with soil to keep her young safe.

That's
Fact-tastic!

Male platypuses have
VENOMOUS SPURS on their
HIND ANKLES. When threatened,
a platypus can **RELEASE** enough
VENOM to **KILL** a **MEDIUM-SIZE
DOG.** Platypuses have **MORE
VENOM** during **BREEDING
SEASON,** so scientists believe
that males use it defend their
mates from rival males.

Echidnas **DON'T HAVE** a
PERMANENT POUCH like a
kangaroo's. Instead, they have
SPECIAL STOMACH MUSCLES
that can squeeze to form a pouch-
like fold. Even male echidnas can
form pouches, though they don't
carry the young. This makes it
DIFFICULT to tell **MALES**
and **FEMALES APART.**

ECHIDNA

Sometimes called spiny anteaters, echidnas are some of Earth's strangest animals. They have spines like a porcupine's and a beak like a bird's. They're venomous. And though they are mammals, they lay eggs—but then hatch them in a pouch!

Echidnas (uh-KID-nuhs) are monotremes, or egg-laying mammals; they are the only members of this group alive today besides the platypus (p. 232). Their most distinctive trait is the spines that cover their bodies. When threatened, echidnas roll up in a ball with the spines poking outward. They are incredibly ancient creatures that have remained essentially unchanged since prehistoric times. There are four echidna species living today, found only in Australia, Tasmania, and New Guinea. They are classified as either "short-beaked" or "long-beaked," but they don't really have beaks at all. What looks like a beak is actually a fleshy, flexible nose.

Like that of a platypus, an echidna's beak is equipped with sensors that can pick up electrical signals coming from its prey of ants, termites, and earthworms. It's also tipped with sensitive nostrils. Echidnas wield this insect-finding instrument to search out the mounds or nests where its prey shelters. Then they use their sharp claws to tear the mound or nest apart and their six-inch (15-cm) tongue to lap up dinner. Like anteaters, echidnas have no teeth. Instead, hard pads on their tongue and the roof of their mouth grind up their food.

Once a year, an adult female echidna lays a grape-size, leathery egg similar to a reptile's. She rolls the egg into a pouch on her belly, where it stays warm and safe. Ten days later, the baby echidna hatches. Smaller than a jellybean, it uses tiny claws to hold on tight to hairs inside the mother's pouch and laps up milk that leaks from glands there. When its spines start to grow in at about two months of age, it leaves the pouch and enters the outside world.

FACTS

SCIENTIFIC NAME Tachyglossidae (family)

GROUP NAME None

SIZE Up to 30 inches (76 cm)

WEIGHT Up to 22 pounds (10 kg)

EATS Ants, termites, earthworms

A **BABY ECHIDNA** is called a **PUGGLE.**

MORE MAMMALS WITH **ARMOR**

Ankylosaurus was a dinosaur built like a tank, with bony plates covering it nearly from head to toe. Fast-forward to today, and a few creatures—such as crocodiles, beetles, and snails—still use this same method of protection. Even more rare are armored mammals like the echidna (p. 234). These unusual animals have hairs modified by evolution into protective plates or quills.

ARMADILLO

The armadillo is the only mammal with a shell. There are about 20 species of armadillo, all of which live in Mexico, Central America, and South America—except for one. That animal, the nine-banded armadillo, is the only armadillo found in the United States. Armadillos are relatives of anteaters (p. 252) and sloths (p. 254). They forage for insects, including ants and termites, using a sharp sense of smell to sniff out their prey, big front claws for digging to find it, and long tongues to slurp it up.

PORCUPINE

Porcupines can have more than 30,000 spikes that cover most of their body. These spikes are actually quills, hairs modified into thick, hard tubes. The quills usually lie flat, but when a porcupine is threatened, it raises them to warn its attacker to back off. If another animal grabs the porcupine anyway, the quills detach and stick in the assailant's skin. Though their name is Latin for "quill pig," porcupines are members of the rodent family. There are more than two dozen species that live across much of North America.

PANGOLIN

It looks more like a living artichoke than an actual animal. But the pangolin is a real (and very unusual!) mammal that lives in Asia and Africa. Pangolins are unrelated to any other mammal and belong to their own family. Instead of hair, they have scales made of keratin, the same material that forms hair and fingernails. The scales overlap each other like a suit of armor and cover nearly the pangolin's entire body. Its scales are so hard that when the pangolin curls up in a ball, even a lion couldn't bite into it.

SPINY MOUSE

These armored African rodents have spikes, but they probably don't use them for defense. The spiny mouse's back is covered with sharp hairs similar to a hedgehog's quills, but they're much softer, likely too soft to inflict damage on a predator. Instead, the spiny mouse has another way to avoid becoming dinner: If grabbed, it can detach some of its skin, which it can later regrow. A few lizards have this ability, but the spiny mouse is the only mammal known to be able to do this.

HEDGEHOG

Hedgehogs, sometimes called pincushions with legs, live in Asia, Europe, and Africa. The hairs on their backs have evolved into a thick layer of quills. Though they look similar to porcupines, the two groups of mammals are not related. Instead, the hedgehog's closest relatives are moles and shrews (p. 64). A hedgehog's quill-less belly is its most vulnerable part, but when it tucks in its head, legs, and tail and curls up, it becomes a spike-covered ball that is difficult for predators to attack.

GIANT PANDA

FACTS

SCIENTIFIC NAME *Ailuropoda melanoleuca*

GROUP NAME None

SIZE Up to 5 feet (1.5 m)

WEIGHT About 300 pounds (136 kg)

EATS Bamboo

The giant panda is a bear, related to other bear species such as brown bears (p. 34) and polar bears (p. 194). And like all other bears, it is a member of the order Carnivora. But the giant panda isn't a carnivore: It's one of the few animals on Earth that eats almost nothing but bamboo. (Though occasionally, it will eat other things such as small mammals, fish, and insects.) That makes the giant panda mostly a vegetarian!

The giant panda's ancestors were carnivores, like the rest of its meat-eating family. So how does the panda survive on a plant-based diet? Bamboo is actually extremely high in protein and low in carbohydrates—much like meat.

Pandas gradually switched to a vegetarian diet about two million years ago. In that time, they evolved adaptations to help them eat large amounts of bamboo, such as strong jaws for chewing tough plant matter and a special protruding wrist bone that acts like a thumb, helping them hold on to bamboo stems. But the panda still has the digestive system of its carnivorous ancestors. While other plant-eaters, such as gorillas (p. 206) and cows (p. 104), have extra-long digestive tracts adapted to extract every bit of nutrition from their tough diet, pandas have a short digestive tract like a wolf's or a bear's. To get enough nutrients from bamboo, pandas must eat an incredible amount of it. They spend at least 12 hours a day eating and consume around 80 pounds (36 kg) of bamboo every day!

Because giant pandas need so much bamboo to survive, they don't live in close company with each other. Pandas are very territorial: If two happen to get too close, they'll growl, swat, and even bite each other. So giant pandas aren't exactly cuddly creatures, though they may look that way!

BABY giant **PANDAS** are **WHITE.**

That's
Fact-tastic!

Giant pandas may be
the **MOST VOCAL** of **ALL** the
BEAR SPECIES. They don't roar
the way a brown bear does.
Instead, **THEY HONK, HUFF,
BARK,** and **GROWL.** They
also make a **BLEAT** sound
similar to that of a baby
goat or lamb.

Today, red pandas **LIVE ONLY** in **SMALL AREAS** of **ASIA.** But **FOSSILS** of an **ANCIENT RELATIVE** of the red panda **DATING** back **FIVE MILLION YEARS** have been **DISCOVERED** in **NORTH AMERICA,** in what is now Washington State and north-eastern Tennessee, U.S.A. At that time, these areas were covered in **RAINY FORESTS** much like the red panda's **MODERN-DAY HABITAT.**

RED PANDA

They have kitten-like faces, dense fur, and fluffy, ringed tails. Like giant pandas, they eat bamboo—but they don't look much like the black-and-white bears. So what kind of mammal are red pandas?

Scientists have argued over this question for years. In 1825, they classified red pandas as members of the raccoon family, based on characteristics of their heads and teeth, along with their ringed tails. Later, it was found that their DNA shared some similarities with members of the bear family, so red pandas were called a type of bear. More recent genetic research has shown that red pandas are actually the only living member of their own family, the Ailuridae.

Red pandas are about the size of a house cat, with big, bushy tails that can be up to 20 inches (51 cm) long. When nights grow chilly, they wrap these tails around their bodies like fluffy blankets. Red pandas live in the mountains of Nepal and northern Myanmar, and into central China. They are acrobats that spend nearly their whole lives in trees, where they forage for bamboo, as well as fruit, acorns, and eggs. Their cinnamon-red coats and cream-colored faces help camouflage them against the red moss and white lichen that cover the tree trunks in their forest homes.

About 90 percent of the red panda's diet is made up of bamboo. Bamboo is tough to digest and is very low in calories. So red pandas eat an enormous amount of it—about 20,000 leaves each day—to survive, according to one study. Like giant pandas, they even have a specialized, extended wrist bone that works like a thumb to help them grasp the stems. They are one of only a few species on Earth that depend mostly on bamboo for their diet.

FACTS

SCIENTIFIC NAME *Ailurus fulgens*

GROUP NAME None

SIZE Up to 26 inches (66 cm) with a tail up to 20 inches (51 cm) long

WEIGHT Up to 20 pounds (9 kg)

EATS Bamboo, fruit, acorns, eggs

The **CHINESE NAME** for the red panda **TRANSLATES** to **"FIRE FOX."**

That's
Fact-tastic!

The Amazon river dolphin is also called the **PINK DOLPHIN** because some individuals can be pink in color. Experts believe the **PINK COLORING COMES FROM SCAR TISSUE** dolphins get from **PLAYING** and **FIGHTING.** They think the murkiness of the water plays a role, too: Dolphins that live in clear waters are **BLEACHED** to a pale pink by the **SUN.**

AMAZON RIVER DOLPHIN

Most of the world's dolphins are marine mammals that swim and frolic in the oceans. But planet Earth is also home to a few dolphins of a different nature. These are the freshwater, or river, dolphins. There are seven species of river dolphin around the world, living in the waterways of Asia and South America. The best-known of them all is the Amazon river dolphin, or boto.

Every year, spring rains cause the Amazon and Orinoco Rivers to spill over their banks and flood thousands of square miles of rainforest. Amazon river dolphins swim into the flooded forest, winding their way between submerged tree trunks. To do this, they have an adaptation not shared by their ocean-dwelling cousins: the ability to bend their necks, which allows them to make tight turns through their underwater jungle. Unlike oceanic dolphins, Amazon river dolphins also have long beaks and bulging foreheads, which help them focus their echolocation clicks and better navigate through murky waters.

To attract mates, male river dolphins are known to grasp branches or grasses in their mouths, then use them to beat the water. Sometimes, they'll hold objects such as pieces of wood or even live turtles high in the air and twirl in circles.

The different species of river dolphin are not related to one another. They evolved on their own from ancestors that swam in the seas and later adapted to life in freshwater. But because of human impacts, the survival of all river dolphins is threatened. These unique marine mammals face many threats, from overfishing of their prey to noise that makes it difficult for them to echolocate. One species, the Yangtze river dolphin, was driven to extinction over the past two decades.

FACTS

SCIENTIFIC NAME *Inia geoffrensis*

GROUP NAME Pod

SIZE Up to 8 feet (2.4 m)

WEIGHT Up to 408 pounds (185 kg)

EATS Fish, shrimp, crabs

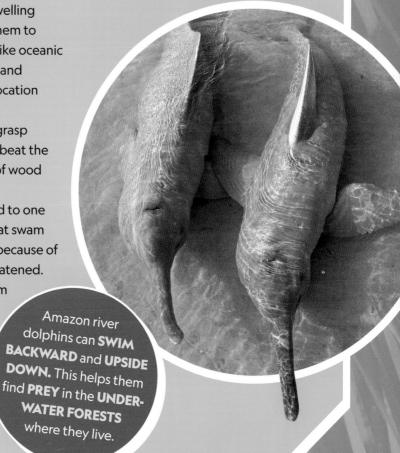

Amazon river dolphins can **SWIM BACKWARD** and **UPSIDE DOWN.** This helps them find **PREY** in the **UNDER-WATER FORESTS** where they live.

MAMMALS THAT FLY

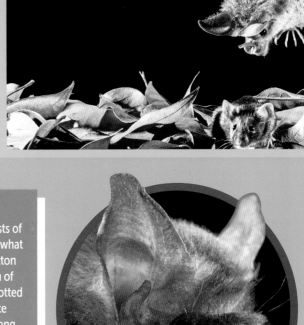

Flying squirrels may be impressive aerial acrobats that can zoom hundreds of feet through the air. But they can't actually fly—only glide. There's only one kind of flying mammal on the planet: bats.

WHITE BAT

If you're visiting the forests of Central America and see what looks like a cluster of cotton balls stuck to the bottom of a leaf, you've actually spotted a group of snoozing white bats. These bats chew along the veins of heliconia plant leaves, causing the leaves to collapse into a sheltering "tent." The bats' white coats help conceal them: When sun shines through their leafy hiding spot, the bats look green.

KITTI'S HOG-NOSED BAT

It's the world's smallest mammal. Sometimes called the bumblebee bat for its miniature size, it weighs just about .07 ounce (2 g)—as much as two Skittles— and can fit on a human fingertip. Scientists know little about the two small populations of them that roost in caves in Thailand and Myanmar. Experts believe the Kitti's hog-nosed bat is the last living member of a bat family called Craseonycteridae, which split from the rest of the bats about 33 million years ago.

VAMPIRE BAT

During the day, vampire bats sleep in total darkness, hanging upside down from the roofs of caves. When night falls, they unfurl their wings and take to the skies. They're hungry, and they only eat one thing: blood! They're the only mammals on Earth that feed only on blood. They use razor-sharp teeth to bite, then slurp up the blood with their tongues. Special chemicals in their saliva prevent it from clotting, keeping the blood flowing so the bats can lap it up. Vampire bats usually prey on horses and cows, but they have been known to bite humans.

GOLDEN-CROWNED FLYING FOX

It's a bat with a wingspan as wide as a human is tall. The golden-crowned flying fox, which flies through the forests of the Philippines, is the largest bat in the world, with wings that can stretch up to 5.5 feet (1.7 m) long. Their wings are so long that these bats often rest with them wrapped around their bodies, like a cloak. That might make this mammal sound like Dracula, but these bats only weigh up to 2.6 pounds (1.2 kg), and they eat only fruit.

MEXICAN FREE-TAILED BAT

These bats are tiny creatures, no bigger than two adult human thumbs pressed together. Yet they are the world's fastest mammalian flyer, capable of reaching nearly 100 miles an hour (161 km/h). They can also reach heights of 10,000 feet (3,000 m) as they swoop through the air while searching for food. Mexican free-tailed bats can eat up to two-thirds of their body weight in insects in a single night. During the day, they sleep in enormous groups called colonies. The largest known colony numbered 20 million bats!

GREATER BULLDOG BAT

Most bats eat insects. But the greater bulldog bat, which flaps its wings from Mexico to South America, has a different sort of diet: Though it does munch on insects, it also catches fish! Using echolocation, the greater bulldog bat can sense the ripples made by fish swimming near the water's surface. It strikes like an eagle, grabbing its prey in its claws and carrying it to a perch for eating.

SOLENODON

FACTS

SCIENTIFIC NAME *Solenodon* (genus)

GROUP NAME None

SIZE About 12 inches (31 cm) with a 10-inch (25-cm) tail

WEIGHT Up to 2.4 pounds (1.1 kg)

EATS Insects, worms, fruit, plants

When a solenodon is **ALARMED**, it frequently **TRIPS** over its **OWN FEET** and takes a **TUMBLE.**

Very few animals were able to survive the asteroid impact that killed off nearly all the dinosaurs—not to mention *also* make it all the way through the next 66 million years to today! Those that have, such as crocodiles and horseshoe crabs, are sometimes called "living fossils," because they have remained almost unchanged for millions of years. Very few mammals can make this claim to fame, but the solenodon is one. And that's not the only strange thing about it.

Solenodons are shrewlike mammals that grow to about a foot (30 cm) long, not including their ratlike tail. The ancestors of the solenodon separated from the ancestors of other placental mammals (such as horses, hares, and humans) about 70 million years ago. That means that this creature has scurried since the Cretaceous period—the time when *Tyrannosaurus rex* roamed Earth. Remarkably, scientists think that when the asteroid hit, solenodons had been making their home near what became the impact site off the coast of Mexico, which means they not only survived—they even survived a direct hit.

Today, there are just two surviving species of solenodon, one living on the island of Cuba and the other on the island of Hispaniola. They are so unlike any other living mammal that these two species form their own biological family, the Solenodontidae. Though they have fur and make milk like other mammals, they have several unusual qualities. Solenodons have a ball-and-socket joint like the one in your shoulder—but theirs is in their snout, enabling them to rotate it. They use echolocation to find prey. And they have a venomous bite, a quality shared by only a handful of mammals on Earth.

Solenodon venom can easily kill creatures such as insects or lizards. There are only a few reports of humans who have suffered the solenodon's toxic bite. They describe symptoms similar to a snake bite, with severe pain that can last days.

That's
Fact-tastic!

Some scientists believe that many **ANCIENT MAMMALS** had **VENOM.** They think most lost this ability as they evolved, but since **SOLENODONS** have remained basically **UNCHANGED** for **MILLIONS** of **YEARS,** they have **REMAINED VENOMOUS.**

That's
Fact-tastic!

After mating, female
BINTURONGS can **PAUSE
THEIR PREGNANCIES,**
delaying them until the time
is right to give birth. This may
sound like a strange ability, but it's
quite common in the animal
kingdom. **MOST CARNIVORES
CAN DO IT,** as well as many
rodents, deer, anteaters,
and armadillos.

BINTURONG

These odd mammals move so slowly through the trees that they are often mistaken for sloths. They have a body similar to a bear's, a face like a cat's, and a tail like a monkey's. They're a member of the carnivore order, but they eat mostly fruit. And they're sometimes called "bearcats," but they're not related to either species. They're binturongs.

Binturongs live in the dense tropical rainforest of Southeast Asia. They use their prehensile tails like an extra limb to help them move through the branches and climb from tree to tree. They're the only mammal in the Old World (Africa, Asia, and Europe) and one of just two carnivores that has a tail like this: The other is the kinkajou (p. 58). Also like kinkajous, binturongs can rotate their ankles 180 degrees. This allows them to use their claws to grip not only when they are climbing up tree trunks but also when they are climbing down.

Binturongs move at a leisurely pace through the treetops as they search for food, foraging in either the day or night. They can do this because binturongs have no natural predators. Binturongs are omnivores that will eat just about anything they come across, from vegetables to birds and even to fish. But they mainly eat fruit, and like many large rainforest fruit-eaters, they help spread seeds from the fruit they eat through their poo.

One thing these animals don't eat is popcorn— but they do smell like it! Binturongs secrete a popcorn-smelling substance from a gland under their tail. As they drag their tail through the trees, they leave a scent trail behind them. This isn't to make the forest smell like a movie theater—it's to communicate with other binturongs.

FACTS

SCIENTIFIC NAME *Arctictis binturong*

GROUP NAME None

SIZE Up to 35 inches (90 cm) with a tail up to 33 inches (84 cm) long

WEIGHT Up to 50 pounds (22 kg)

EATS Fruit, vegetables, insects, eggs, fish

A binturong's **TAIL** has a **LEATHERY PATCH** at the tip to give it **EXTRA GRIP.**

RABBITS AND THEIR RELATIVES

Rabbits are rodents ... aren't they? Scientists certainly thought so until the early 20th century. But though they have incisor teeth that never stop growing, all rodents have only two incisors on the top and two on the bottom. Rabbits and their relatives have four on the top and four on the bottom. These animals—rabbits, hares, and pikas—make up their own family, the lagomorphs.

EASTERN COTTONTAIL

Cottontail rabbits, named for their "cotton ball" tail, live from Canada all the way to South America. They have large eyes high on the sides of their heads. That gives these rabbits 360 degrees of vision, except for a small blind spot directly in front of them. If you face one of these rabbits head-on, it will turn its head to the side so it can see you. When it does, you might also notice it twitching its nose. Eastern cottontails have millions of scent sensors in their noses, and the wiggling motion helps them pick up smells.

BLACK-TAILED JACKRABBIT

These animals commonly hop through American deserts, scrublands, and other open spaces. They're incredibly speedy for their small size, able to reach 40 miles an hour (64 km/h), and use their powerful hind legs to make leaps of more than 10 feet (3 m). They use their speed and a zigzag way of moving to evade coyotes and other predators.

ILI PIKA

With its face resembling a teddy bear's, it may be the most adorable of all the lagomorphs. It lives high in the remote mountains of northwestern China, where it was only discovered in 1983. Since then, it's been spotted only a few times, and very little is known about it. This extra-furry pika is a cousin of the American pika; those lagomorphs can be found only in North America and Asia.

ARCTIC HARE

While animals such as bears get through the winter season by hibernating, arctic hares survive the cold in other ways. They are able to eat woody plants, mosses, and lichens, which many other animals can't survive on. Their thick fur helps keep them warm, along with their compact body and shortened ears. In winter, that fur turns brilliant white, making the hares hard to spot against ice and snow. When spring begins, their coat turns to a blue-gray color that helps them blend in with the rocks around them.

VOLCANO RABBIT

This animal gets its name from its extreme habitat: It lives mainly on the slopes of four extinct volcanoes near Mexico City, Mexico. Weighing just about a pound (0.5 kg), it's one of the world's smallest rabbits. Volcano rabbits depend on a certain species of tall, dense grass that grows on the sides of their volcano homes. It helps the rabbits hide from predators such as weasels (p. 54) and bobcats (p. 29). Volcano rabbits are endangered; experts estimate there are fewer than 7,000 of them in the wild.

AMERICAN PIKA

They're the smallest members of the lagomorph group, at just about eight inches (20 cm) long. Experts believe that ancestors of the American pika lived in Siberia and traveled across a land bridge that once existed between Asia and Alaska. Today, American pikas live in rocky slopes of the western United States. In the summer, when food is plentiful, pikas collect grasses and wildflowers and lay them in the sun to dry. Then they store them in their dens for winter.

That's
Fact-tastic!

They may not look
like it, but giant anteaters
are **EXCEPTIONALLY GOOD
SWIMMERS.** They use the
freestyle stroke and can
BREATHE by using their
LONG SNOUT as a **SNORKEL.**
They have been observed
crossing wide rivers
this way.

GIANT ANTEATER

What has no teeth but can eat up to 30,000 ants in a day? An anteater, of course! Anteaters are among the few mammals in the world with no teeth. This small group, called the Xenarthra (ZEN-ar-thra), includes anteaters, tree sloths, and armadillos.

Anteaters feed on nothing besides ants and termites, and their bodies are specially adapted to the job: They walk on their fists with their long claws curled up, which helps keep them sharp for digging out insects. Their long, narrow nose is perfect for poking into ant and termite mounds. Their two-foot (60-cm)-long tongue is shaped like a strand of spaghetti and covered with backward-facing barbs and sticky saliva to help grab on to ants.

Giant anteaters eat by darting their tongue in and out of mounds up to 150 times per minute. They feed at each mound for only about a minute. That keeps them from wiping out an entire colony, so they can come back for more later. Once an anteater has a mouthful of ants or termites, it crushes them against the roof of its mouth. It has a muscular stomach that grinds up its food even more.

There are four anteater species, and the giant anteater is the largest. From the tip of its snout to the end of its tail, it can be longer than an adult human is tall! Most female anteaters have a single baby, called a pup, each year. Sometimes, anteater pups ride around on their mother's back.

FACTS

SCIENTIFIC NAME *Myrmecophaga tridactyla*

GROUP NAME None

SIZE Up to 4 feet (1.2 m) with a tail up to 35 inches (89 cm) long

WEIGHT Up to 140 pounds (64 kg)

EATS Ants, termites

Anteaters sometimes use their large, **BUSHY TAIL** as **SHELTER** from **RAIN** or **SUN**.

SLOTH

FACTS

SCIENTIFIC NAME Folivora (suborder)

GROUP NAME Bed

SIZE Up to 29 inches (74 cm)

WEIGHT Up to 20 pounds (9 kg)

EATS Shoots, leaves, fruit

BROWN-THROATED THREE-TOED SLOTH

It takes a sloth up to a **MONTH** to **DIGEST** a **MEAL**.

From pronghorns (p. 76) to cheetahs (p. 32) to Mexican free-tailed bats (p. 245), many mammals are among the speediest animals on Earth. Not the sloth. This animal moves so slowly that algae actually grows on its fur! It's the slowest mammal there is.

There's a reason "slothful" is another word for "lazy": Sloths sleep up to 18 hours a day! Even when they're awake, they spend much of their time motionless. They are active for just a short time each night, when they eat leaves, shoots, and fruit. Experts once thought sloths had no teeth, like their cousins the anteaters (p. 252). But they actually do have teeth, just not very many! They have 10 upper teeth and eight lower teeth. Their two front teeth are used for biting off their food, and the rest of their teeth are flat and used for grinding up food.

Sloths spend nearly their entire lives upside down in the trees. In fact, the only time they come down to the forest floor is to poo, which they do about once a week. Because of their upside-down lifestyle, sloths have hair that grows in the opposite direction from the hair of all other mammals—it parts in the middle of their belly and grows toward their back. This helps rain run off the sloth's body during rainstorms. Each strand of a sloth's fur is grooved, an adaptation that encourages algae to grow on the fur. This gives sloths a greenish tint, helping them hide among the leaves.

There's one other trait that sets sloths apart from the rest of the mammals: their body temperature. Whereas most mammals maintain a constant body temperature, a sloth's temperature can range from 74°F (24°C) to 92°F (33°C). If your body temperature changed that much, it would mean that you're sick! But for sloths, it's a way to conserve energy.

That's Fact-tastic!

Hang upside down for a while and you might notice that it becomes hard to breathe. That's because organs such as your liver and stomach press down on your lungs when in this position. **SLOTHS** don't have this problem—they have **SPECIAL MEMBRANES** that **ATTACH** their **ORGANS** to their **BONES** so that they can **BREATHE EASILY** when **UPSIDE DOWN.**

LINNAEUS'S TWO-TOED SLOTH

That's
Fact-tastic!

Colugos have unusual teeth. Their lower front teeth are divided into long points, forming a shape that looks like a comb. Colugos appear to use these teeth for **SCRAPING EDIBLE MORSELS** off **TREE BARK** and also for **GROOMING** their **FUR.**

COLUGO

Is it a bat? A flying squirrel? Neither. This little-known creature is called a colugo. To make matters more confusing, it's sometimes known as a flying lemur—but it's not a lemur, and it can't really fly. Instead, it glides. And it's the most skilled gliding mammal on Earth, able to soar an incredible 230 feet (70 m) from tree to tree. That's about as long as the wingspan of a jumbo jet!

Like flying squirrels (p. 150), colugos soar by stretching out a thin membrane of skin. But this membrane, also called a patagium, is the most extensive of any gliding animal's: It stretches all the way around the animal, from its face to the tips of its claws. That basically makes the colugo a living kite and gives it incredible gliding power. The patagium also attaches to the colugo's tail. Female colugos fold the bottom of their patagium over and use it as a pouch for holding their babies. When it's time to drift off to a new tree, colugo mothers are so good at gliding that they can even carry their babies with them. Little colugos cling to their mom as she sails around the forest. What a wild ride!

There are at least two species of colugo, but experts think there are likely more. Their large red eyes give them sharp night vision, which helps them navigate when gliding between trees in the darkness of night, when they are active. During the day, colugos grab on to tree trunks or hang upside down from branches and snooze, relying on their gray-brown fur to help them blend into the forests of their Southeast Asia home.

Colugos split off from the rest of the mammals about 80 million years ago. They are so different from all other mammals that they not only form their own family group, Cynocephalidae, but also their own order, Dermoptera. (Other mammal orders include Carnivora and Rodentia.) Colugos are not related to other gliding mammals such as flying squirrels. Their closest living relatives are actually primates!

FACTS

SCIENTIFIC NAME Cynocephalidae (family)

GROUP NAME None

SIZE Up to 16 inches (40 cm)

WEIGHT About 4 pounds (1.8 kg)

EATS Leaves, shoots, fruit

There are more than **60 SPECIES** of **GLIDING MAMMALS** alive today.

EXTINCT ODD MAMMALS

Ever since paleontologists started digging up fossils, they have been discovering baffling creatures. That's no surprise: The Earth is about 4.5 billion years old—plenty of time for some truly bizarre animals to evolve and then go extinct. These are some of the most unusual mammals that have ever shared our planet.

MACRAUCHENIA

This South American mammal had a neck like a llama's, a body like a horse's, three-toed feet like a rhino's, and possibly a trunk like a tapir's. So what was it? Scientists puzzled over *Macrauchenia* fossils for nearly two centuries, until they found a rare surviving DNA sample. It showed that the mystery mammal was part of a unique group most closely related to horses, rhinos, and tapirs.

MEGATHERIUM

Modern sloths are small animals, averaging around 11 pounds (5 kg). But this ancient sloth species was bigger—much, much bigger! *Megatherium,* the giant ground sloth, stood 23 feet (7 m) tall and weighed as much as an elephant. Far too heavy to hang from trees, *Megatherium* slunk across the ground in North and South America. It lived until very recently, going extinct just about 12,000 years ago. Giant sloth fossils have been found with cut marks on them, suggesting that ancient humans once hunted them.

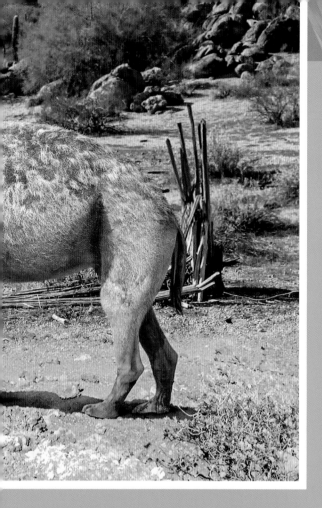

ARSINOITHERIUM

It looked like a rhinoceros with two horns instead of one. But *Arsinoitherium* was actually not directly related to the rhino. Instead, its closest living cousins are elephants. This 10-foot (3-m)-long ancient herbivore lived in parts of what are now Africa and the Middle East about 30 million years ago, where it probably ate water plants, mangroves, and other vegetation. Paleontologists believe its double horns weren't for fighting but for attracting mates.

SYNTHETOCERAS

One set of horns wasn't enough for *Synthetoceras tricornatus.* This bizarre, deerlike animal roamed North America about 10 million years ago. *Synthetoceras* had a set of horns above its eyes similar to those of many horned animals living today. But on its snout, it grew a second, longer horn with a forked tip. Because only males had these forked horns, experts think they were probably used for fighting over territories. No members of its family have survived to the modern day.

THYLACOSMILUS

It was an ancient sabertooth—but it wasn't a cat. *Thylacosmilus atrox,* an extinct mammal that roamed South America about six million years ago, was actually a kind of marsupial the size of a jaguar. Because it sported enormous canine teeth nearly identical to those of the saber-toothed cat *Smilodon,* experts long assumed it was a fearsome predator, too. Now they believe it was more likely to be a scavenger that dined on the leftovers of other killers.

259

A TALK WITH CHRISTINE WILKINSON

Christine Wilkinson grew up watching squirrels and subway rats in her hometown of New York City. Now she tracks spotted hyenas in Kenya, Africa. Wilkinson is a mammologist, or scientist who studies mammals, at the University of California, Berkeley. We spoke with her to find out more about what these keen observers of animals do.

WHAT DO MAMMOLOGISTS DO?

There are so many mammals of all different sizes and shapes, of course—even including humans! And there are just as many different ways to be a mammologist. Some of us study how mammals evolve. Others work on the biology of what's going on inside of mammals. Others—like me—work on conservation, or helping to protect mammals and their environments.

WHAT MADE YOU WANT TO STUDY MAMMALS?

I grew up in Queens, New York, where I didn't have very many mammals around. But I loved climbing trees, and up in the trees I found a lot of squirrels. They were the first mammals that I fell in love with. I also found the New York City subway rats really clever, and I was always amazed by how well they could survive. I loved to watch them on the subway tracks. One year, the city cleaned the entire subway, which meant that there were way fewer rats afterward. I remember feeling really sad about that. But now, as a scientist, I study the same concept: How human activity is affecting a different species— the spotted hyena.

WHAT'S YOUR FAVORITE MAMMAL?

My favorite mammals are my dog, River, and my cat, Merlin, of course! But my favorite mammal species is the one I study: the spotted hyena. They are super adaptable. They are so clever that they have even outperformed chimpanzees on intelligence tests. The females are bigger than the males, and they are in charge of hyena societies. Hyenas have jaws so strong they can crush bone, and bodies that can digest it. They are amazing animals!

HOW DO YOU STUDY SPOTTED HYENAS?

I study human-carnivore conflict—in other words, how carnivores sometimes attack livestock or pose other risks to people, and how the people respond. Hyenas are often involved in human-carnivore conflict; if they have the opportunity, they will sometimes prey on sheep and other livestock animals. Because humans depend on these livestock animals to survive, they will sometimes get back at the hyenas. That puts spotted hyenas at risk.

I track spotted hyenas in Kenya, Africa. The hyenas are outfitted with special collars that allow me to watch their movements using GPS. In the area where I work, there is a national park with a fence surrounding it. It's supposed to be impossible to get through—but by using remote cameras, I can watch as the hyenas I'm tracking twist and contort their bodies to get right through the fence!

WHAT DO YOU HOPE TO ACCOMPLISH?

My ultimate goal is to help hyenas and humans coexist. I have found that the best way to do that is to put the right tools in the hands of the people who need them. One tool is predator-proof enclosures where people can keep their livestock at night, when hyenas are on the prowl. Another is these boxes that give off light and sound that people can put on an enclosure to scare away hyenas.

It's also important to look at the situation from the humans' side, not just the hyenas'. For example, many of the folks in the area where I work are dealing with poverty. They are much less likely to survive a livestock attack if they count on just a few animals for milk, meat, and a paycheck. To protect hyenas, we have to tackle the poverty problem, too.

WHY SHOULD PEOPLE CARE ABOUT HYENAS?

Besides the fact that they are super fascinating, hyenas are essential to the health of their ecosystem. They are an apex predator, which means that they are really important for helping the entire food chain survive and thrive. For example, where I work, there is an area where farmers raise 6,000 cattle. The cattle have to graze the ecosystem alongside wild herbivores, like gazelles and zebras. Without hyenas around to prey on these herbivores, their population would grow out of control, and they would eat all the grass, leaving nothing for the cattle. Hyenas are essential for making sure there is enough food for all species to survive.

On top of that, hyenas are nature's cleanup crew. They scavenge carcasses, getting rid of every bit down to the hair and bone. It's very likely that in doing so, they are protecting people from bacteria that could make them or their livestock sick. That's something that's really unusual and special about hyenas. Hyenas have another unique trait: They appear to sometimes not be affected in the usual ways by certain diseases, such as anthrax and rabies. Scientists are currently studying this ability, and someday, hyenas may help us discover new treatments for disease.

WHAT ADVICE WOULD YOU GIVE TO KIDS WHO WANT TO STUDY MAMMALS?

Go outside and try to find your local squirrels, voles, or mice. Sit down on the ground in the early morning and right before dusk, when these animals are most active, and watch their behavior. The more you go, the more you'll notice patterns in what they do. When you get home, research what you saw. Later on, you can read books and take biology classes. But don't be afraid to start your mammalogy research right now!

SPOTTED HYENAS

GLOSSARY

ADAPTATIONS: physical or behavioral changes that happen gradually to help a species survive in its environment

AQUATIC: living all or most of the time in water

ARBOREAL: living in or often found in trees

CAMOUFLAGE: an organism's ability to disguise its appearance, often by changing its coloring or body shape to blend in with its surroundings

CANOPY: the highest level of a forest, formed by the tops of the tallest trees

CARNIVORES: animals that survive by eating other animals

CLASSIFICATION: grouping based on physical and genetic characteristics

CONSERVATIONIST: a person who works to protect the environment, wildlife, and natural resources

WESTERN GRAY KANGAROOS

CREPUSCULAR: active mostly during twilight

DIURNAL: active mostly during the day

DOMESTICATED: species that have been tamed over many generations, such as dogs and cows

ECHOLOCATION: a sensory system in some animals in which sounds are produced and their echoes interpreted to figure out the direction and distance of objects. Bats and dolphins use echolocation to navigate and find food.

ECOSYSTEM: community and interactions of living and nonliving things in an area

ECTOTHERM: an animal that does not keep its internal body temperature above that of the environment, so it moves into or out of the heat as needed; commonly referred to as "cold-blooded"

ENDANGERED: relating to an animal or plant that is found in such small numbers that it is at risk of becoming extinct, or no longer existing

ENDOTHERM: an animal that keeps its internal body temperature above that of the environment, usually within a narrow range; commonly referred to as "warm-blooded"

EVOLVE: to change gradually over long periods of time

EXOTHERMIC: an animal that relies on its surroundings to regulate its body temperature

FORAGE: to search for food

WILD BOAR PIGLETS

HABITAT: a place in nature where an organism lives throughout the year or for shorter periods of time

HIBERNATION: the process of reducing activity almost to sleeping to conserve food and energy, usually in winter

MAMMARY GLAND: the part of the female body that makes milk for baby mammals to drink

MATRIARCHAL: a community run by females

MIGRATION: process in which a community of organisms leaves a habitat for part of the year or part of their lives, and moves to another habitat that is more hospitable

NOCTURNAL: active during the night

OPPOSABLE: capable of being placed opposite something else, as in the opposable thumb, which can be placed opposite the fingers on the same hand, allowing objects to be picked up

PLACENTA: an organ in most mammals that develops during pregnancy and nourishes an unborn baby

POPULATION: a group of living things of the same species that live in a particular place

PREDATOR: an animal that survives mostly by hunting and eating other animals

PREHENSILE: able to grasp something by wrapping around it, as in a prehensile tail

PREY: an animal that is hunted and eaten by other animals

PRIMITIVE: a species that has changed very little over many generations

SCAVENGER: organism that eats dead or rotting flesh

SCRUBLAND: an area of land covered with low trees and bushes

SPECIES: a group of similar organisms that can reproduce with one another

TAIGA: forest land just south of the Arctic, where lots of pine trees and other conifers grow; also called the boreal forest

TORPOR: a state of very low brain and body activity that occurs in some mammals when food is scarce

TUNDRA: cold, treeless areas that lie between the permanent ice of the Arctic and the northern forests of North America, Europe, and Asia

FIND OUT MORE

SEA OTTER

BOOKS

Amazing Evolution: The Journey of Life
by Anna Claybourne

DK Eyewitness Books: Mammal by Steve Parker

Explorer: Mammals! by Nick Forshaw

*National Geographic Illustrated Guide to Wildlife:
From Your Back Door to the Great Outdoors*
by Catherine Herbert Howell

*National Geographic Kids Ultimate Explorer Field
Guide: Mammals* by Patricia Daniels

National Geographic Prehistoric Mammals
by Alan Turner

Smithsonian Handbooks: Mammals
by Juliet Clutton-Brock

WEBSITES

A note for parents and teachers: For more
information about mammals, you can visit these
websites with your young readers.

Discover endangered mammals at the World
Wildlife Fund's website.

Ooh and aah over adorable baby mammals and
more at ZooBorns.

Play animal games at Switch Zoo.

Meet the marine mammals being rehabilitated at
the Pacific Marine Mammal Center and watch them
live on a webcam.

Read profiles of a huge variety of mammals on the
National Geographic Kids website.

MOVIES & TV

African Wild [2011]: Get up close with the animals
of Africa

Big Cat Diary [1996]: This long-running show takes
a fun look at big cats in Kenya's Masai Mara National
Reserve

Feeding Time [2011]: Watch animals chow down in
zoos across the United States and United Kingdom

The Life of Mammals [2002]: David Attenborough
narrates this 10-episode series that takes an
in-depth look at mammals from shrews to whales

Up Close and Natural [2012]: This PBS show was
created to inspire young students to appreciate the
natural world

*Wild America: Mysterious and Marvelous
Mammals* [2009]: This 10-part series takes viewers
on a journey across the United States to learn about
its native mammals

PLACES TO VISIT

The Academy of Natural Sciences of Drexel University in Philadelphia, Pennsylvania

American Museum of Natural History in New York City

Beaty Biodiversity Museum in Vancouver, Canada

Field Museum of Natural History in Chicago, Illinois

Natural History Museum in London, U.K.

Smithsonian Institution National Museum of Natural History in Washington, D.C.

HOFFMANN'S TWO-TOED SLOTHS

SEA LIONS

GRIZZLY BEARS

INDEX

INDEX

PHOTO CREDITS

AD=Adobe Stock; AL=Alamy Stock Photo; GI=Getty Images; IS=iStockphoto; NGIC=National Geographic Image Collection; SS=Shutterstock

Front Cover: (kangaroo), Dirk Freder/E+/GI; (orca), Tory Kallman/SS; (grizzly bear), Design Pics/NGIC; (harp seal), Coulanges/SS; (hedgehog), Viorel Sima/AD; (orangutan), Eric Isselee/SS; (giant panda), Eric Isselee/SS; (leopard), Londolozi Images/Mint Images RF/GI; (background), Integral/AD; **Spine:** (tiger), MrPreecha/AD; (baboon), Eric Isselee/Dreamstime; **Back Cover:** (armadillo), Luis/AD; (ring-tailed lemur), yakub88/AD; (wolf), Jess R. Lee; **Back Flap:** (UP), Stephanie Drimmer; (LO), Celeste Sloman; **Background Textures:** (sheep fur), majeczka/SS; (tiger fur), PhotoDisc; (giraffe fur), Integral/AD Photo; (manatee skin), Vladimir Wrangel/AD Photo; (baboon fur), ondrejprosicky/AD Photo; (leopard fur), byrdyak/AD Photo; (elephant skin), gmackenzie/AD Photo; (capybara fur), maljalen/AD Photo; (porcupine quills), Nazzu/AD Photo; **Front Matter:** 1, Tony Heald/SS/Nature Picture Library; 2-3, Roland Seitre/Minden Pictures; 3 (hedgehog), Viorel Sima/AD; 3 (giant panda), Eric Isselee/SS; 4 (UP LE), JackF/AD Photo; 4 (LO LE), Steve Winter/NGIC; 4 (UP RT), dpa picture alliance archive/AL; 4 (LO RT), Delbars/SS; 5 (UP), Paul Nicklen/NGIC; 5 (CTR), Life on white/AL; 5 (LO), Tratong/SS; 6 (UP), Celeste Sloman; 6 (CTR), Wayne Marinovich/SS; 6 (LO), ArCaLu/SS; 7 (UP), Stephanie Drimmer; 7 (LO), Jim Abernethy/NGIC; **Chapter One:** 8-9, kyslynskahal/SS; 10 (UP), Craig Dingle/SS; 10 (CTR), Chris Minihane/GI; 10 (LO), Nick Fox/SS; 11 (UP), Beverly Joubert/NGIC; 11 (CTR), Alex Mustard/AL; 11 (LO LE), Gerry Ellis and Karl Ammann/Digital Vision; 11 (LO RT), Four Oaks/SS; 12 (UP), Eyal Bartov/AL; 12 (LO), Dave Watts/AL; 12-13, Tomas Dardos/SS; 13 (LE), Andrii Piantychka/SS; 13 (RT), John Giustina/GI; 14, Tuan Dao/GI/500px; 15 (UP LE), Beverly Joubert/NGIC; 15 (UP RT), Jim Cumming/AL; 15 (LO), Design Pics Inc/NGIC; 16 (UP), Mindy Fawver/AL; 16 (CTR), Rudmer Zwerver/SS; 16 (LO), FloridaStock/SS; 17 (UP), Jo Reason/SS; 17 (LO), Ondrej Prosicky/SS; 18 (UP), ZSSD/Minden Pictures; 18 (LO), Steve Bloom Images/AL; 19 (UP), Wirestock Creators/SS; 19 (CTR), Jiri Haureljuk/SS; 19 (LO), Satheesh Rajh Rajagopalan/AL; 20 (LE), Michael Long/Science Photo Library; 20 (RT), Graham Prentice/AL; 20 (LO), Gudkov Andrey/SS; 20-21, Franco Tempesta; 21, Brian Lasenby/SS; 22 (UP), PetStockBoys/AL; 22 (LO), Friedrich von Horsten/AL; 23 (UP), John Hyde/Design Pics Inc/AL; 23 (CTR LE), Lucas Barros/GI/IS; 23 (CTR RT), Agami Photo Agency/SS; 23 (LO), Juergen Ritterbach/AL; 24 (coyote), Jim Cumming/SS; 24 (wolverine), Popova Valeriya/SS; 24 (jaguar), Anan Kaewkhammul/SS; 24 (two-toed sloth), Eric Isselee/SS; 24 (blue whale), 3drenderings/AD; 24 (elephant seal), Jurgen & Christine Sohns/GI/ImageBroker RF; 24 (bottlenose dolphin), Neirfy/SS; 25 (narwhal), dottedyeti/AD; 25 (polar bear), Uryadnikov Sergey/AD; 25 (red fox), Eric Isselee/SS; 25 (moose), Photosvac/AD; 25 (Siberian tiger), Apple-2499/AD; 25 (giant panda), Isselee/Dreamstime; 25 (red kangaroo), Bradley Blackburn/AD; 25 (koala), Eric Isselee/SS; 25 (African lion), Eric Isselee/SS; 25 (reticulated giraffe), Eric Isselee/

SS; 25 (African savanna elephant), Talvi/SS; **Chapter Two:** 26-27, Steve Winter/NGIC; 28, Nigel Dennis/imageBROKER/AL; 28-29, Brian Skerry/NGIC; 29 (UP LE), Jeffrey Lepore/Science Source; 29 (UP RT), Wildestanimal/SS; 29 (LO), Ondrejprosicky/AD; 30, Andy Rouse/SS/Nature Picture Library; 31, Calum Agnew/GI/EyeEm; 32, Vaganundo Che/SS; 32-33, Mary Ann McDonald/GI; 33 (UP), Bobs Creek Photography/SS; 33 (LO LE), Grant Ordelheide/GI/Aurora Open; 33 (LO CTR), Koilee/SS; 33 (LO RT), Leonardo Mercon/SS; 34, Paul Souders/GI; 35, Dgwildlife/GI/IS; 36, Marc Moritsch/NGIC; 37, Animals Animals/NGIC; 38 (LE), Jackie Connelly-Fornuff/SS; 38 (RT), Kevin Le/SS; 38-39, Arndt Sven-Erik/Arterra Picture Library/AL; 39 (UP), Mauro Toccaceli/AL; 39 (LO), Ondris/SS; 40, Andrew Kandel/AL; 41, Tom Murphy/NGIC; 42, Jim Kruger/GI; 43, Jim and Jamie Dutcher/NGIC; 44, Ozkan Ozmen/AL; 44-45 (UP), Tami Freed/AL; 44-45 (LO), Will Burrard-Lucas/Nature Picture Library/AL; 45 (UP), Andrew Davies/AL; 45 (LO), Stu Porter/AL; 46, NaturesMomentsuk/SS; 47, Enrique Aguirre Aves/GI; 48, Arco G. Lacz/AL; 49, Suzi Eszterhas/Minden Pictures; 50, Manoj Shah/GI; 50-51, Londolozi Images/GI/Mint Images RF; 51 (UP), Jim and Jamie Dutcher/NGIC; 51 (LO), Jim and Jamie Dutcher/NGIC; 52, Blickwinkel/AL; 53, AGAMI Photo Agency/AL; 54 (UP), James Hager/Robert Harding/AL; 54 (LO), Robin Joyce/SS; 54-55, Krys Bailey/AL; 55 (UP LE), Somogyi Laszlo/SS; 55 (UP RT), mlorenzphotography/GI; 55 (LO), Cordier Sylvain/Hemis/AL; 56, Bruno D'Amicis/Nature Picture Library/AL; 57, Zoltan Molnar/AL; 58, Neil Bowman/GI/IS; 59, Photoshoot/Avalon.red/AL; 60 (LE), Bildagentur Zoonar GmbH/SS; 60 (RT), Ondrej Prosicky/SS; 60-61, Danita Delimont/SS; 61 (LE), Charlie Hamilton James/NGIC; 61 (RT), Phototrip/AL; 62, Vikram Singh/imageBROKER/AL; 63, Olga Rudneva/AL; 64, Theo Douma/CAGAMI Photo Agency/AL; 65, Blickwinkel/AL; 66 (LE), Roman Uchytel/Prehistoric Fauna; 66 (RT), Ryan Rosotto/NGIC; 67 (UP), Jamie Chirinos/Sceience Photo Library; 67 (LO LE), Daniel Eskridge/GI/IS; 67 (LO RT), Daniel Eskridge/Stocktrek Images, Inc/AL; **Chapter Three:** 68-69, Federico Cabello/SuperStock/AL; 70, Watchara Manusnanta/AD; 71 (UP), Budimir Jevtic/AD; 71 (LO LE), JohanSwanepoel/AD; 71 (LO RT), Igor Pushkarev/AD; 72, Gunter Nuyts/SS; 73, Beverly Joubert/NGIC; 74, Image BROKER/SS; 75, Gudkov Andrey/SS; 76, Danita Delimont/SS; 76-77, Jared Lloyd/GI; 77 (UP), WILDLIFE GmbH/AL; 77 (LO), Mari Swanepoel/SS; 78, Jeff R Clow/GI; 79, Rudi Hulshof/SS; 80, Kevin Schafer/GI; 81, GFC Collection/AL; 82 (UP), Johan Swanepoel/SS; 82 (CTR), Pi_Kei/SS; 82 (LO), Foto-master/AD; 83 (UP), Rich Legg/GI; 83 (LO), Thanakorn Hongphan/SS; 84, Dominique Braud/Dembinsky Photo Associates/AL; 85, Doug Lindstrand/Design Pics Inc/AL; 86, WILDLIFE GmbH/AL; 86-87, Todd Grimsley/SS; 87, Patrick J. Endres/GI; 88, Slowmotion-gli/SS; 89, Slowmotiongli/SS; 90, Loflo69/SS; 91, Acon Cheng/SS; 92, Rick Strange/AL; 92-93, Jochen Tack/AL; 93 (UP), Dmitry Pichugin/SS; 93 (alpacas), Lialina/SS; 93 (llamas), Noe Besso/SS; 93 (guanacos), Ron Watts/GI; 93 (vicuñas), Sabine_lj/SS; 94, Timmy V Photography/SS; 95, Robert Harding/NGIC; 96, Cornelius Doppes/SS; 97, Andrew Kandel/AL; 98 (LE), Johan Swanepoel/SS; 98 (RT), Rosanne Tackaberry/AL; 99 (UP LE),

Dominyk Lever/SS; 99 (UP RT), Images of Africa Photobank/AL; 99 (LO LE), Yakov Oskanov/SS; 99 (LO RT), Taranukhin Alex/AD; 100, Joe Blossom/AL; 101, Joe Blossom/AL; 102, Ondrej Prosicky/SS; 103, Ann and Steve Toon/AL; 104, Clara Bastian/AD; 105 (UP LE), Anne Coatesy/SS; 105 (UP RT), Rita_Kochmarjova/SS; 105 (LO LE), Linas T/SS; 105 (LO RT), Tony Campbell/SS; 106, Mark A. McCaffrey/SS; 107, Doug Lindstrand/Design Pics Inc/AL; 108 (LE), National Geographic Partners, LLC; 108 (RT), Science History Images/AL; 109 (UP LE), Michael Long/Science Photo Library; 109 (UP RT), Ryan Risotto/NGIC; 109 (LO), National Geographic Partners,LLC; **Chapter Four:** 110-111, Suzi Eszterhas/Minden Pictures; 112, Gerry Ellis/Minden Pictures; 112-113, Konrad Wothe/Minden Pictures; 113 (LE), Ger Bosma/GI; 113 (RT), Bill Hatcher/NGIC; 114, Freder/GI; 115, Jami Tarris/GI; 116, CraigRJD/GI/IS; 117, CraigRJD/GI/IS; 118 (UP), Wirestock Creators/SS; 118 (LO), B.G. Thomson/Science Source; 119 (UP LE), Jean-Paul Fererro/AL; 119 (LO LE), Ken Griffiths/SS; 119 (RT), Tracie Louise/GI/IS; 120, Slowmotiongli/GI/IS; 121, Mark Newman/GI; 122 (UP), EF Volart/GI; 122 (LO), Sander Groffen/AD; 123 (UP), Jean-Paul Fererro/AL; 123 (LO), C. Huetter/AL; 124, Juergen & Christine Sohns/Minden Pictures; 125, Blickwinkel/AL; 126, Dave Watts/AL; 127, Martin Harvey/GI; 128 (UP), Anom Harya/SS; 128 (LO), Gerhard Koertner/Avalon.red/AL; 128-129, Jason Edwards/GI; 129 (LE), Stephanie Jackson, Australian wildlife collection/AL; 129 (RT), Daryl Dickson; 130, Jonas Boernicke/SS; 131, Posnov/GI; 132, Holly Kuchera/SS; 133, Jay Ondreicka/SS; 134 (LE), Will Meinderts/NGIC; 134 (RT), Philippe Psaila/Science Photo Library; 135 (UP), Leonardo Mercon/SS; 135 (LO LE), Anton Sorokin/AL; 135 (LO RT), Mark Chappell/AGE Fotostock; 136, S.Rohrlach/GI/IS; 137, Michael Willis/AL; 138 (UP), Vac1/GI/IS; 138 (LO), National Geographic Partners, LLC; 139 (UP), National Geographic Partners, LLC; 139 (CTR), Adrie & Alfons Kennis/NGIC; 139 (LO), Mauricio Anton/Science Photo Library; **Chapter Five:** 140-141, Westend61/SS; 142 (UP), Gabriel Rojo/AL; 142 (LO), Raphael Sane/BIOSPHOTO/AL; 143 (UP LE), Anthony Bannister/Avalon.red/AL; 143 (UP RT), Sander Meertins/AD; 143 (LO), Eumates/SS; 144, Paul Souders/AD; 145, Jose A. Bernat Bacete/GI; 146, Thomas Sbampato/imageBROKER/AL; 147, George Lepp/GI; 148, Octavio Campos Salles/AL; 149, Therin Weise/AL; 150 (UP), Stan Tekiela/GI; 150 (LO), Jeff Mangiat/Mendola Ltd; 151 (UP LE), Joel Sartore/NGIC; 151 (UP RT), London Zoological Society Public Domain; 151 (LO), Jeff Mangiat/Mendola Ltd; 152, Blickwinkel/AL; 153, Roland Seitre/Minden Pictures; 154 (UP), Elementals/SS; 154 (LO), Svitlana Zarytska/SS; 154-155 (UP), Miroslav Hlavko/SS; 154-155 (LO), Billion Photos/SS; 155 (LE), DenVIP/SS; 155 (RT), Mary Swift/SS; 156, Michael Durham/Minden Pictures; 157, Rick & Nora Bowers/AL; 158, HenkBentlage/GI/IS; 158-159, Radius Images/Design Pics/AL; 159 (UP), Albert Beukhof/SS; 159 (CTR), Paulpixs/SS; 159 (LO), Colacat/SS; 160, John Cancalosi/NGIC; 161, Jak Wonderly/NGIC; 162 (LE), Millard H. Sharp/Science Source; 162 (RT), National Geographic Partners, LLC; 163 (UP), Marcio Castro; 163 (LO LE), Christian Darkin/Science Photo Library; 163 (LO RT), April Neander; **Chapter Six:** 164-165, Milo Burcham/Design Pics Inc/AL; 166-167 (UP), Keith Ladzinski/NGIC; 166-167 (LO), Peter Verhoog/Buiten-beeld/Minden Pictures; 167 (UP), DK Images/Science Photo Library; 167 (LO), A.G. Owen/AD; 168, Mark Carwardine/Nature Picture Library; 169, Hiroya Minakuchi/Minden Pictures; 170 (UP), WaterFrame/AL; 170 (LO LE), Paul Souders/GI; 170 (LO RT), WILDLIFE GmbH/AL; 171 (UP), Tomas Kotouc/SS; 171 (LO LE), HeitiPaves/GI/IS; 171 (LO RT), Wildestanimal/AL; 172, Norbert Probst/imageBROKER/AL; 173, Stephen Frink/GI; 174, Brian Skerry/NGIC; 174-175 (UP), Paul Nicklen/NGIC; 174-175 (LO), Chase Dekker/SS; 176, Verlisia/GI/500px; 177, Milo Burcham/Design Pics Inc/AL; 178, Cory Richards/NGIC; 179, Enric Sala/NGIC; 180, Danny Ye/AL; 180-181, National Geographic Partners, LLC; 181, Skinfaxi/

GI/IS; 182, Paul Nicklen; 183, Paul Nicklen; 184, Doptis/SS; 185, Pascal Kobeh/Nature Picture Library; 186-187, Brian Skerry/NGIC; 187 (LO LE), Whale Research Solutions/NGIC; 187 (LO RT), Brian Skerry/NGIC; 188, Dominique Braud/Dembinsky Photo Associates/AL; 189, Tobias Friedrich/AL; 190, Erin Donalson/SS; 191, Robert Harding/NGIC; 192, Brian Skerry/NGIC; 193, Brian Skerry/NGIC; 194, Johnny Johnson/GI; 195, Andy Mann/NGIC; 196, Roman Uchytel/Science Photo Library; 196-197, Roman Uchytel/Science Photo Library; 197 (UP), National Geographic Partners, LLC; 197 (CTR), Roman Uchytel/Prehistoric Fauna; 197 (LO), Rushelle Kucala; **Chapter Seven:** 198-199, Wonderlasts in Reality/GI; 200, Thomas Marent/Minden Pictures; 201 (UP LE), Thomas Marent/Minden Pictures; 201 (UP RT), W. Otero Fotografía/AD; 201 (LO LE), Rolf Nussbaumer Photography/AL; 201 (LO RT), Tao Jiang/AD Photo; 202, Don Mammoser/SS; 203, Jeff Mauritzen/NGIC; 204 (LE), Cyril Ruoso/Minden Pictures; 204 (UP RT), Blickwinkel/AL; 204 (LO RT), Andrey Gudkov/SS; 205 (UP), StRa/SS; 205 (LO), Gerdie Hutomo/SS; 206, Robert Harding Picture Library/NGIC; 207, Gudkov Andrey/AD; 208 (UP), Suzi Eszterhas/Minden Pictures; 208 (LO), Michael Nichols/NGIC; 209 (UP), Michael Nichols/NGIC; 209 (LO), Joel Sartore/NGIC; 210, Edwin Butter/AD; 211, Teekayu/SS; 212, Ackats/SS; 213, Peter Houlihan/NGIC; 214, Ondrej Prosicky/GI/IS; 215, David Tipling Photo Library/AL; 216, Frans Lanting/NGIC; 216-217, Cheryl-Ramalho/SS; 217 (UP), Peter Houlihan/NGIC; 217 (LO LE), Sneil375/GI/IS; 217 (LO RT), 4FR/GI/IS; 218, 4FR/GI; 219, Erni/SS; 220, Wollertz/AD; 221, Ger Bosma/GI; 222, Anup Shah/GI; 222-223, Natalia Paklina/SS; 223 (UP LE), Edwin Butter/SS; 223 (UP RT), Houdin and Palanque/Nature Picture Library/AL; 223 (LO), Javarman/SS; 224, Hkhtt Hj/SS; 225, Binturong Tonoscarpe/SS; 226 (LE), Xijun Ni/Chinese Academy of Sciences; 226 (UP RT), Xijun Ni, Chinese Academy of Sciences; 226 (LO RT), Julius T. Csotonyi/Science Photo Library; 227 (UP), John Sibbick/Science Photo Library; 227 (CTR LE), Joseph McNally/NGIC; 227 (CTR RT), Robert Clark/NGIC; 227 (LO LE), Sabena Jane Blackbird/AL; 227 (LO RT), Dave Einsel/GI; **Chapter Eight:** 228-229, Volodymyr Burdiak/AL; 230, Lauren/AD; 231 (UP LE), Jurgen & Christine Sohns/imageBROKER/AL; 231 (UP RT), Pal Hermansen/Nature Picture Library; 231 (LO LE), mgkuijpers/AD; 231 (LO RT), Charlie Hamilton James/NGIC; 232, Robin Smith/GI; 233, Doug Gimesy/Nature Picture Library; 234, Xavier Hoenner Photography/GI; 235, Dave Watts/AL; 236, Marcelo Morena/SS; 236-237 (UP), Fabian von Poser/imageBROKER/AL; 236-237 (LO), Teekayu/SS; 237 (UP), Itsik Marom/AL; 237 (LO), Supakrit Tirayasupasin/SS; 238, Katherine Feng/NGIC; 239, Ami Vitale/NGIC; 240, Gui00878/GI/IS; 241, Freder/GI; 242, Sylvain Cordier/GI; 243, Flip Nicklin/NGIC; 244 (LE), Don Mammoser/SS; 244 (RT), Merlin Tuttle; 244-245, Anand Alluri Varma/NGIC; 245 (UP), Bill Coster/GI; 245 (CTR), Michael Durham/Nature Picture Library/AL; 245 (LO), Frans Lanting/NGIC; 246, Joel Sartore/NGIC; 247, Science History Images/AL; 248, Arco TUNS/Imagebroker/AL; 249, MrPreecha/AD; 250 (UP), Rabbitti/SS; 250 (LO), Twildlife/GI/IS; 251 (UP LE), Bebedi/AL; 251 (UP RT), Daboost/GI/IS; 251 (LO LE), Li Weidong; 251 (LO RT), Marina Poushkina/SS; 252, Panoramic Images/AL; 253, ondrejprosicky/AD; 254, Damsea/SS; 255, Michael Nitzschke/imageBROKER/AL; 256, David Yeo/AL; 257, Attapol/AD; 258, National Geographic Partners, LLC; 258-259, Roman Uchytel/Science Photo Library; 259 (UP), Mark Turner/AL; 259 (CTR), Jaime Chirinos/Science Photo Library; 259 (LO), Lucas Lima/Paleostock; **Back Matter:** 260, Jessica Ortiz; 261, Uwe Skrzypczak/AL; 262, Suzi Eszterhas/Minden Pictures; 263, Duncan Usher/Minden Pictures; 264, Nathan Pang/SS; 265 (UP), Suzi Eszterhas/Minden Pictures; 265 (LO LE), Joost van Uffelen/SS; 265 (LO RT), Design Pics Inc/NGIC; 272, WILDLIFE GmbH/AL

For Sloane, my favorite mammal —S.W.D.

Copyright © 2023 National Geographic Partners, LLC

All rights reserved. Reproduction of the whole or any part of the contents without written permission from the publisher is prohibited.

NATIONAL GEOGRAPHIC and Yellow Border Design are trademarks of the National Geographic Society, used under license.

Since 1888, the National Geographic Society has funded more than 14,000 research, conservation, education, and storytelling projects around the world. National Geographic Partners distributes a portion of the funds it receives from your purchase to National Geographic Society to support programs including the conservation of animals and their habitats. To learn more, visit natgeo.com/info.

For more information, visit nationalgeographic.com, call 1-877-873-6846, or write to the following address:

National Geographic Partners, LLC
1145 17th Street NW
Washington, DC 20036-4688 U.S.A.

For librarians and teachers: nationalgeographic.com/books/librarians-and-educators

More for kids from National Geographic:
natgeokids.com

National Geographic Kids magazine inspires children to explore their world with fun yet educational articles on animals, science, nature, and more. Using fresh storytelling and amazing photography, *Nat Geo Kids* shows kids ages 6 to 14 the fascinating truth about the world—and why they should care. **natgeo.com/subscribe**

For rights or permissions inquiries, please contact National Geographic Books Subsidiary Rights: bookrights@natgeo.com

Designed by Amanda Larsen and Mary Wages

The publisher would like to acknowledge the following people for making this book possible: Stephanie Warren Drimmer, author; Angela Modany, editor; Jen Agresta, project editor; Lisa M. Gerry, editor; Amanda Larsen, art director; Lori Epstein, photo manager; Matt Propert, photo editor; Mary Wages, designer; Alix Inchausti, senior production editor; Gus Tello, designer; Michelle Harris, fact-checker.

The publisher would also like to thank Dr. Rae Wynn-Grant for her expert review of the manuscript.

Library of Congress Cataloging-in-Publication Data

Names: Drimmer, Stephanie Warren, author.
Title: Ultimate mammalpedia / by Stephanie Warren Drimmer.
Description: Washington, D.C. : National Geographic Kids, [2023] I Includes index. I Audience: Ages 7-10 I Audience: Grades 2-3
Identifiers: LCCN 2021044580 I ISBN 9781426373213 (hardcover) I ISBN 9781426374494 (library binding)
Subjects: LCSH: Mammals--Encyclopedias--Juvenile literature.
Classification: LCC QL701.2 .D75 2023 IDDC 599/.03--dc23
LC record available at https://lccn.loc.gov/2021044580

Printed in Hong Kong
23/PPHK/1

RED PANDA